TRIO
WRITING 1

**The Intersection of
Vocabulary, Grammar, & Writing**

Alice Savage & Colin Ward

OXFORD
UNIVERSITY PRESS

OXFORD
UNIVERSITY PRESS

198 Madison Avenue
New York, NY 10016 USA

Great Clarendon Street, Oxford, ox2 6dp, United Kingdom

Oxford University Press is a department of the University of Oxford.
It furthers the University's objective of excellence in research, scholarship,
and education by publishing worldwide. Oxford is a registered trade
mark of Oxford University Press in the UK and in certain other countries

Director, ELT New York: Laura Pearson

Head of Adult, ELT New York: Stephanie Karras

Publisher: Sharon Sargent

Managing Editor: Tracey Gibbins

Executive Art and Design Manager: Maj-Britt Hagsted

Content Production Manager: Julie Armstrong

Design Project Manager: Lisa Donovan

Image Manager: Trisha Masterson

Senior Image Editor: Fran Newman

Production Coordinator: Christopher Espejo

ISBN: 978 0 19 485400 9 Student Book 1 with Online Practice Pack
ISBN: 978 0 19 485401 6 Student Book 1 as pack component
ISBN: 978 0 19 485402 3 Online Practice website

Printed in China

This book is printed on paper from certified and well-managed sources

ACKNOWLEDGEMENTS

Illustrations by: Ben Hasler, pg. 20, 44, 58, 96, 120; Paul Williams, pg. 32, 46, 47,
70, 82, 87, 108; 5W (maps), pg. 58, 63, 68.

*We would also like to thank the following for permission to reproduce the following
photographs:* pg.vi Shutterstock; pg.1 Syda Productions/Shutterstock, Mike
Zarrilli/Getty Images Sport, Neale Cousland/Shutterstock; pg. 3 East/
Shutterstock, archideaphoto/iStock, Katerina Planina/Shutterstock,
Image Source/OUP, WDG Photo/Shutterstock, OlegDoroshin/Shutterstock,
Intellistudies/iStock, Matelly/Getty Images; pg. 4 Cynthia Farmer/Shutterstock,
ene/Shutterstock, Jeffrey Coolidge/Corbis, ra2studio/Shutterstock, Space
Chimp/Shutterstock, East/Shuttersotck, Matelly/Getty Images, nadiya_sergey/
shutterstock, WDG Photo/Shutterstock; pg. 5 Ditty_about_summer/
Shutterstock, Hero Images/Corbis, B.A.E. Inc./Alamy, Ocean/Corbis, Mike
Zarrilli/Getty Images Sport, Radiokafka/Shutterstock, waklla/iStock, Echo/
Getty Images, Innocenti and Lee/Image Source/Corbis; pg. 6 Ocean/Corbis,
bo1982/iStock, Andrey_Popov/Shutterstock, Mike Zarrilli/Getty Images
Sport, Tara Moore/Getty Images, oleg/66/iStock, Andrey_Popov/Shutterstock,
Syda Productions/Shutterstock; pg. 7 Jaak Nilson/Spaces Images/Corbis,
David Grossman/Alamy, LilliGraphie/Shutterstock, Ollyy/Shutterstock,
Tips Images/Alamy, Olga Kovalenko/Shutterstock, Brian Jackson/Alamy,
Hemerocallis/Shutterstock, B.A.E. Inc./Alamy, pagedesign/iStock, Neale
Cousland/Shutterstock, OlegDoroshin/Shutterstock; pg. 8 Alibi Productions/
Alamy, Maxisport/Shutterstock, twohumans/iStock, Mirko Pernjakovic/
iStock, Bloomburg/Getty Images, digieye/Shutterstock, edwardmallia/iStock,
Igor Klimov/Shutterstock; pg. 9 Steven Frame/Shutterstock, cute vector/
Shutterstock, KIM NGUYEN/Shutterstock, windu/Shutterstock, PhotosIndia.
com LLC/Alamy, Roger Browning/Shutterstock; pg. 19 Blue Images/Corbis,
Blend Images/Getty, luna4/Shutterstock; pg. 21 My Good Images/Shutterstock,
Blue Images/Corbis, Altrendo Images/Getty Images, Simon Marcus/Corbis, IM_
photo/Shutterstock, Tetra Images/Alamy; pg. 22 Jenny Matthews/Alamy, Diego
Cervo/Shutterstock; pg. 33 MJTH/Shutterstock, Blend Images-Kidstock/Alamy,
Dann Tardif/LWA/Corbis, 68/Ocean/Corbis, Ocean/Corbis, Vikulin/Shutterstock,
wavebreakmaedia/Shutterstock; pg. 57 Sergey A. Kravchenko/Shutterstock,
237/Sam Edwards/Ocean/Corbis, Image Source/Alamy; pg. 59 Nataly Lukhanina/
Shutterstock, Xiong Wei/Shutterstock, Laborant/Shutterstock, peter zelei/
iStock, Caro/Alamy, jessicakirsh/Shutterstock; pg. 60 Bareta/iStock, Tibor
Bognar/Corbis; Matej Hudovernik/Shutterstock, JanRoode/iStock; pg. 61 All
Canada Photos/Alamy, Melvyn Longhurst/Alamy, D Core/Ocean/Alamy, skvoor/
Shutterstock, TANZANIANIMAGES/iStock; pg. 64 Ditty_about_summer/
Shutterstock; pg. 71 arek_malang/Shutterstock, mura/iStock, Pawel Gaul/
Getty Images, Gavin Hellier/Agefotostock; pg. 73 Ray Roberts/Alamy; pg. 83
Alexander Sherstobitov/Shutterstock, nullplus/iStock, Flip Nicklin/Minden
Pictures/Corbis, EuropeanLandmarksandTravel/OUP; pg. 84 Levent Konuk/
Shutterstock, Juice Images/Alamy; pg. 95 Mark Sykes/Alamy, Jose Fuste Raga/
Corbis, Maridav/Shutterstock; pg. 97 leaf/iStock, Twin Design/Shutterstock,
Andrew Aitchison/In Pictures/Corbis, Goodluz/Shutterstock; pg. 109 oksix/
Shutterstock, Begovic, Damir/Agefotostock, Lewis Tse Pui Lung/Shutterstock,
andresr/iStock, Eddie Gerald/Alamy; pg. 110 Photolibrary/OUP, Directphoto/
Agefotostock, paul prescott/Shutterstock; pg. 112 Brian Jannsen/Alamy; pg.
121 Hill Street Studios/Gary Kious/Getty Images, Odua Images/Shutterstock,
Picture Press/Alamy, ImageBROKER/Alamy, Michael Prince/Corbis, Florin Stana/
Shutterstock, Radu Bercan/Shutterstock,BC.

REVIEWERS

We would like to acknowledge the following individuals for their input during the development of the series:

Aubrey Adrianson
Ferris State University
U.S.A.

Sedat Akayoğlu
Middle East Technical University
Turkey

Lisa Alton
University of Alberta
Canada

Türkan Aydin
Çanakkale Onsekiz Mart University
Turkey

Pelin Tekinalp Cakmak
Marmara University, School of Foreign
Languages
Turkey

Karen E. Caldwell
Zayed University
U.A.E.

Danielle Chircop
Kaplan International English
U.S.A.

Jennifer Chung
Gwangju ECC
South Korea

Elaine Cockerham
Higher College of Technology
Oman

Abdullah Coskun
Abant Izzet Baysal University
Turkey

Linda Crocker
University of Kentucky
U.S.A.

Adem Onur Fedai
Fatih University Preparatory School
Turkey

Greg Holloway
Kyushu Institute of Technology
Japan

Elizabeth Houtrow
Soongsil University
South Korea

Shu-Chen Huang
National Chengchi University
Taipei City

Ece Selva Küçükoğlu
METU School of Foreign Languages
Turkey

Margaret Martin
Xavier University
U.S.A.

Murray McMahon
University of Alberta
Canada

**Shaker Ali Mohammed
Al-Mohammadi**
Buraimi University College
Oman

Eileen O'Brien
Khalifa University of Science,
Technology and Research
U.A.E.

Fernanda Ortiz
Center for English as a Second
Language at University of Arizona
U.S.A.

Ebru Osborne
Yildiz Technical University
Turkey

Joshua Pangborn
Kaplan International
U.S.A.

Erkan Kadir Şimşek
Akdeniz University Manavgat
Vocational College
Turkey

Veronica Struck
Sussex County Community College
U.S.A.

Clair Taylor
Gifu Shotoku Gakuen University
Japan

Melody Traylor
Higher Colleges of Technology
U.A.E.

Sabiha Tunc
Baskent University English Language
Department
Turkey

John Vogels
Dubai Men's College
U.A.E.

Author Acknowledgments

We would like to thank the many people who were involved in the development of *Trio Writing*, which began over Mexican food in Houston, where the idea for it was born in a meeting with Sharon Sargent, our friend and guide throughout this long process. Sharon, thank you for believing in us.

We are indebted to our brilliant editorial team: Tracey Gibbins, Mariel DeKranis, Keyana Shaw, Karin Kipp, and Anita Raducanu. We'd also like to give a special thanks to Stephanie Karras, who has been instrumental in bringing the idea to fruition.

Finally, we'd like to thank our friends and families, Margi Wald for sharing ideas and resources, our spouses Stefanie and Masoud who good-naturedly endured the endless beep of text messages as we sent ideas back and forth, and our children who made their own snacks when we were on a roll. It has been a wonderful journey, and we are very grateful to have had such fantastic fellow travelers.

—A. S. and C. W.

CONTENTS

Welcome to Trio Writing

Building Better Writers...From the Beginning

Trio Writing includes three levels of Student Books, Online Practice, and Teacher Support.

Level 1/CEFR A1

Level 2/CEFR A2

Level 3/CEFR B1

Essential Digital Content

iTools DVD-ROM with Classroom Resources

Trio Writing weaves together contextualized vocabulary words, grammar skills, and writing strategies to provide students with the tools they need for successful academic writing at the earliest stages of language acquisition.

Vocabulary Based On the Oxford 2000 ✎ Keywords

Trio Writing's vocabulary is based on the 2,000 most important and useful words to learn at the early stages of language learning, making content approachable for low-level learners.

Explicit, Contextualized Skills Instruction

Contextualized Grammar Notes and Writing Strategies are presented to teach the most useful and relevant skills students need to achieve success in their writing.

Readiness Unit

For added flexibility, each level of *Trio Writing* begins with an optional Readiness Unit to provide fundamental English tools for beginning students.

INSIDE EACH CHAPTER

▲ VOCABULARY

Theme-based chapters set a context for learning.

Essential, explicit skills help beginning learners to generate independent academic writing.

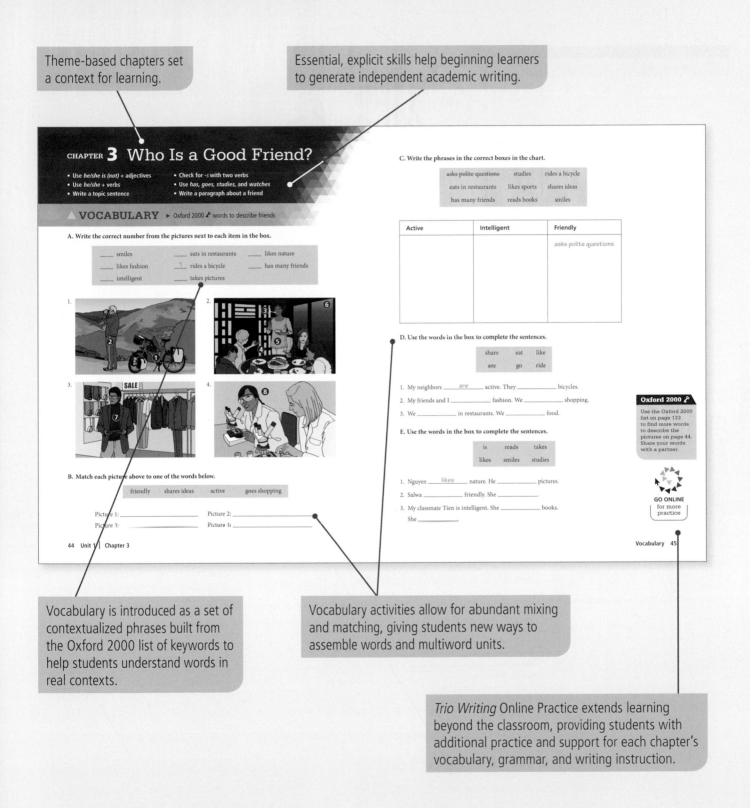

CHAPTER **3** Who Is a Good Friend?

- Use *he/she is (not)* + adjectives
- Use *he/she* + verbs
- Write a topic sentence
- Check for *-s* with two verbs
- Use *has, goes, studies,* and *watches*
- Write a paragraph about a friend

▲ **VOCABULARY** ► Oxford 2000 ✐ words to describe friends

A. Write the correct number from the pictures next to each item in the box.

____ smiles   ____ eats in restaurants   ____ likes nature
____ likes fashion   _1_ rides a bicycle   ____ has many friends
____ intelligent   ____ takes pictures

1.
2.
3. SALE
4.

B. Match each picture above to one of the words below.

friendly   shares ideas   active   goes shopping

Picture 1: _____   Picture 2: _____
Picture 3: _____   Picture 4: _____

44   Unit 1 | Chapter 3

C. Write the phrases in the correct boxes in the chart.

asks polite questions   studies   rides a bicycle
eats in restaurants   likes sports   shares ideas
has many friends   reads books   smiles

Active	Intelligent	Friendly
		asks polite questions

D. Use the words in the box to complete the sentences.

share   eat   like
are   go   ride

1. My neighbors ____*are*____ active. They _____ bicycles.
2. My friends and I _____ fashion. We _____ shopping.
3. We _____ in restaurants. We _____ food.

E. Use the words in the box to complete the sentences.

is   reads   takes
likes   smiles   studies

1. Nguyen ____*likes*____ nature. He _____ pictures.
2. Salwa _____ friendly. She _____.
3. My classmate Tien is intelligent. She _____ books.
   She _____.

Oxford 2000 ✐

Use the Oxford 2000 list on page 133 to find more words to describe the pictures on page 44. Share your words with a partner.

GO ONLINE
for more
practice

Vocabulary   45

Vocabulary is introduced as a set of contextualized phrases built from the Oxford 2000 list of keywords to help students understand words in real contexts.

Vocabulary activities allow for abundant mixing and matching, giving students new ways to assemble words and multiword units.

Trio Writing Online Practice extends learning beyond the classroom, providing students with additional practice and support for each chapter's vocabulary, grammar, and writing instruction.

▲▲ GRAMMAR

A two-part grammar presentation with sentence-building practice recycles key vocabulary.

Achievable writing models provide examples of grammar skills in the context of each chapter's writing assignment.

Each grammar lesson contains two Grammar Notes, which are matched closely to the writing task for supportive grammar instruction.

Sentence-building charts provide structure while allowing students options to generate independent writing.

Vocabulary and Grammar Chants found online help students internalize the target grammar structure and vocabulary for greater accuracy and fluency when writing.

▲▲▲ WRITING

After providing practice with a variety of sentence types, *Trio Writing* guides students to generate meaning within and across sentences in the form of a longer writing task.

The Writing lesson builds on the first two lessons by bringing the language and theme together in a six-step, scaffolded writing task. Even the earliest-level language learners are able to create a portfolio of academic writing with *Trio Writing*.

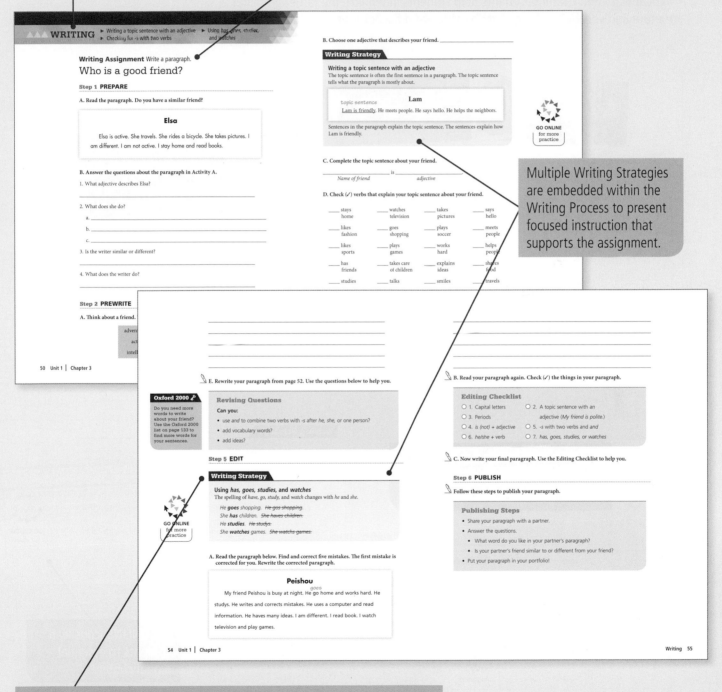

Multiple Writing Strategies are embedded within the Writing Process to present focused instruction that supports the assignment.

Writing Strategies feature additional language points and writing skills so that students become aware of paragraph organization, including main ideas and support, coherence devices, mechanics, spelling, and punctuation.

Trio Writing Online Practice: Essential Digital Content

With content that is exclusive to the digital experience, *Trio Writing* Online Practice provides multiple opportunities for skills practice and acquisition—beyond the classroom and beyond the page.

Each unit of *Trio Writing* is accompanied by a variety of automatically graded activities. Students' progress is recorded, tracked, and fed back to the instructor.

Vocabulary and Grammar Chants help students internalize the target grammar structure and vocabulary for greater accuracy and fluency when writing.

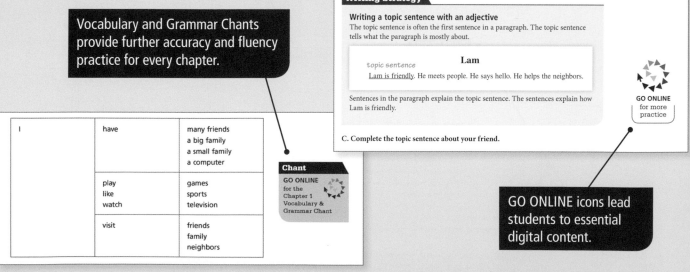

Vocabulary Oxford 2000 words to describe travel plans
Choose *summer* or *winter* to complete each sentence.

1. The weather is cold in the [summer / winter].
2. People wear warm clothes in the [ ].
3. People like cold drinks in the [ ].
4. It snows in the [ ].
5. People complain about hot weather in the [ ].

Reset   Submit

> Online Activities provide essential practice of Vocabulary, Grammar, and Writing Strategies.

> Vocabulary and Grammar Chants provide further accuracy and fluency practice for every chapter.

I	have	many friends
		a big family
		a small family
		a computer
	play	games
	like	sports
	watch	television
	visit	friends
		family
		neighbors

Chant
GO ONLINE for the Chapter 1 Vocabulary & Grammar Chant

Writing Strategy

Writing a topic sentence with an adjective
The topic sentence is often the first sentence in a paragraph. The topic sentence tells what the paragraph is mostly about.

topic sentence
Lam
Lam is friendly. He meets people. He says hello. He helps the neighbors.

Sentences in the paragraph explain the topic sentence. The sentences explain how Lam is friendly.

GO ONLINE for more practice

C. Complete the topic sentence about your friend.

> GO ONLINE icons lead students to essential digital content.

Use the access code on the inside back cover to log in at **www.oxfordlearn.com/login**.

Readiness Unit

Words

Letters
Numbers
Nouns
Verbs
Adjectives

Sentences

Subjects and Verbs
Capital Letters and Periods
Sentences with Nouns and Adjectives
Questions

Paragraphs

UNIT WRAP UP ## Extend Your Skills

▲ WORDS

Letters

The English alphabet has 26 letters. Letters are CAPITAL and lowercase.

CAPITAL: A B C D E F G H I J K L M N O P Q R S T U V W X Y Z

lowercase: a b c d e f g h i j k l m n o p q r s t u v w x y z

Letters form words.

Letters	b o o k	s e v e n	t e n
Words	book	seven	ten

Write the missing letters.

A _B_ __ D __ F __ H I __ K L __ N O __ Q __ S T __ V __ __ Y __

_a_ b c __ __ __ __ g __ i j __ l m __ o p __ r s __ u __ w x __ z

Numbers

Numbers tell how many.

1 one	2 two	3 three	4 four	5 five
6 six	7 seven	8 eight	9 nine	10 ten

Complete the chart.

●●●	3	*three*	●●●●●●●● ●●	9	
●●●●	4		●●●●●●	6	
●	1		●●●●●●●	7	
●●●●●● ●●●●	10		●●	2	
●●●●●	5		●●●●●● ●●	8	

Nouns

Some words are nouns. Nouns are people, places, and things.

People	Places	Things
a student	*a classroom*	*a picture*
a teacher	*a park*	*a phone*

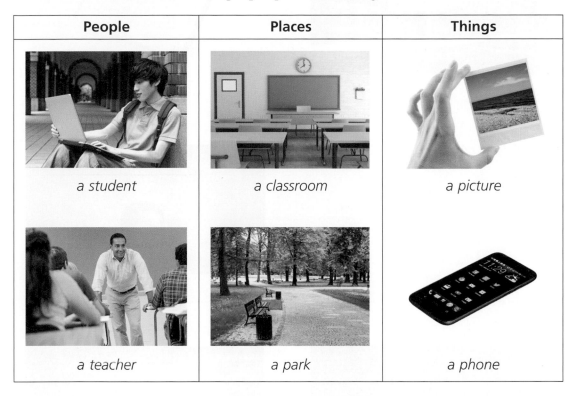

one noun = singular

two or more nouns = plural

a student

students

A. Rewrite the nouns.

1.

park _____ *park* _____

2.

friends _____

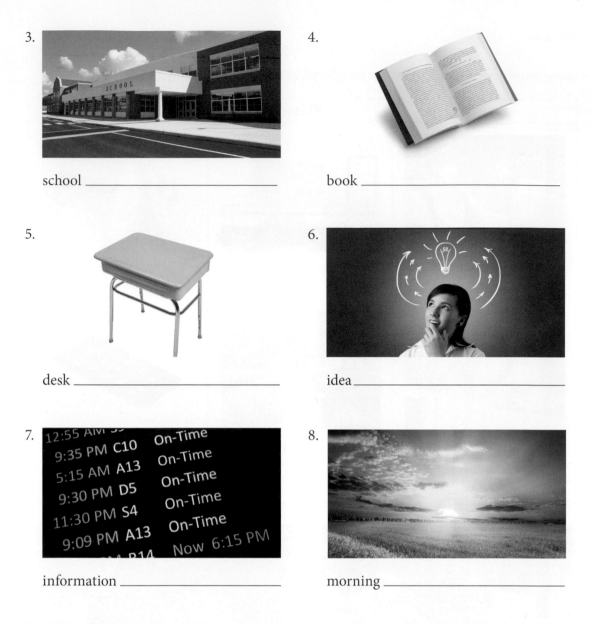

3.

school _____

4.

book _____

5.

desk _____

6.

idea _____

7.

information _____

8.

morning _____

B. Write the correct nouns.

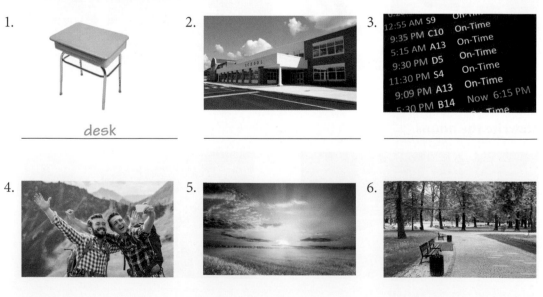

1.

desk

2.

_____

3.

_____

4.

_____

5.

_____

6.

_____

Verbs

Some words are verbs. Verbs describe actions. Some verbs give information.

Actions		Information
I write.	*I read* a book.	*I am* a student.
I use a computer.	*I play* soccer.	*I have* many books.
I study English.	*I explain* ideas.	*I like* pictures.

A. Write the words in the correct boxes in the chart.

computer   friend   have   like   read   park   phone   school   use   write

Nouns	Verbs
computer	

B. Circle the correct verbs to describe the pictures. Then write the sentences.

1.

I   *am*   a computer

     (*use*)

        I use a computer.

2.

I   *write*   a book

     read

3.

I   *write*   information

     explain

4.

I   *play*   soccer

     am

5.

I   *use*   a phone

     like

Adjectives

Some words are adjectives. Adjectives describe nouns.

Adjectives with people		
a **happy** teacher	a **good** student	**my** friends

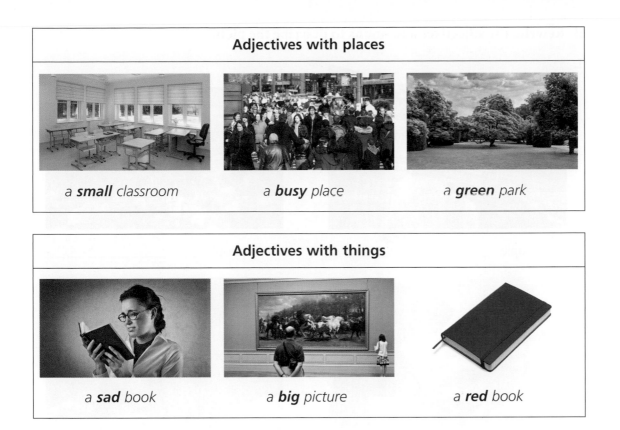

Adjectives with places

a **small** classroom   a **busy** place   a **green** park

Adjectives with things

a **sad** book   a **big** picture   a **red** book

A. Circle the correct adjectives to describe the pictures. Then write the words.

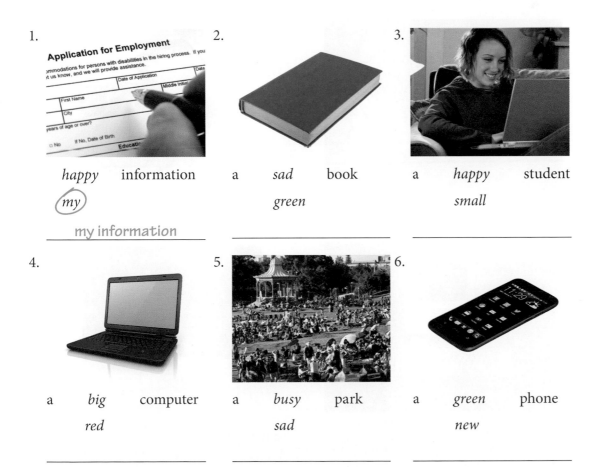

1.
happy information
(*my*)

my information

2.
a   *sad*   book
    green

_____

3.
a   *happy*   student
    small

_____

4.
a   *big*   computer
    red

_____

5.
a   *busy*   park
    sad

_____

6.
a   *green*   phone
    new

_____

B. Rewrite the adjectives and nouns to describe the pictures.

1.

few people _____*few people*_____   many people _____

2.

an interesting book _____   a boring book _____

3.

similar phones _____   different phones _____

4.

an old computer _____   a new computer _____

C. Circle the correct adjectives to describe the pictures. Then write the words.

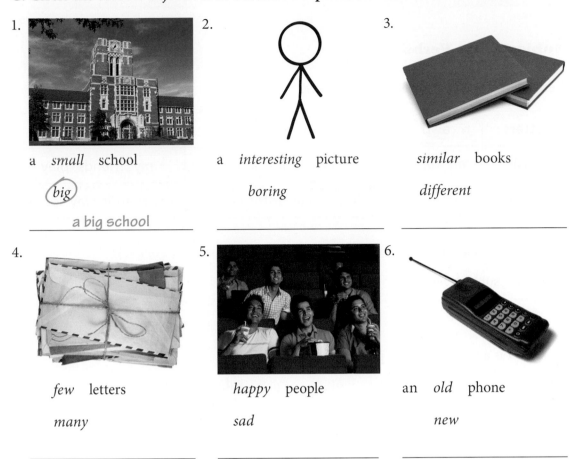

1.
a *small* school
(big)

a big school

2.
a *interesting* picture
boring

3.
similar books
different

4.
few letters
many

5.
happy people
sad

6.
an *old* phone
new

D. Write the words in the correct boxes in the chart.

a book	friends	explain	green	information	a school
a teacher	happy	read	different	like	study
big	play	listen	interesting	pictures	old
a student	a desk	write	similar	busy	walk

Adjectives	Nouns	Verbs
big	a book	play

▲▲ SENTENCES

Subjects and Verbs

Letters form words. Words form sentences.

Letters	h a p p y	h a v e	f r i e n d s
Words	am happy	have information	my friends play
Sentences	I am happy.	Books have information.	My friends play soccer.

A sentence has a subject and a verb.

subject verb
I write.

subject verb
My friends read.

A subject is a noun such as a person, a place, or a thing.

subject (person)
My teacher uses many words.

subject (place)
My classroom is small.

subject (thing)
My phone has pictures.

Read the sentences. Circle the subjects. Underline the verbs.

1. I write new ideas.

2. My friends play soccer.

3. I study English.

4. Teachers use books.

5. People like interesting information.

6. I am busy.

7. My classmates read books.

8. I have an old computer.

Capital Letters and Periods

A sentence begins with a capital letter. A sentence ends with a period.

capital letter   **period**   **capital letter**   **period**

Students read books.   *My school has many classrooms.*

Write the sentences. Use a capital letter and period in each sentence.

1. i have many friends

   I have many friends. _____

2. my phone is green

   _____

3. i like soccer

   _____

4. students have different ideas

   _____

5. computers use information

   _____

6. i have interesting friends

   _____

7. teachers read many books

   _____

Sentences with Nouns and Adjectives

A sentence has a subject and a verb. Sometimes a sentence has more words after a verb.

Sentences with adjectives	Sentences with nouns	Sentences with adjectives and nouns
My friend is busy. *My school is big.*	*My classmates use computers.* *My teacher likes books.*	*I have a good idea.* *Students use many books.*

A. Look at the underlined word(s) in each sentence. Is it an adjective, a noun, or both? Choose the correct answer.

1. I have a <u>phone</u>.
   a. adjective
   b. noun ⟵(circled)
   c. adjective and noun

2. My teacher is <u>good</u>.
   a. adjective
   b. noun
   c. adjective and noun

3. My school has <u>many teachers</u>.
   a. adjective
   b. noun
   c. adjective and noun

4. I am <u>happy</u>.
   a. adjective
   b. noun
   c. adjective and noun

5. I like <u>new computers</u>.
   a. adjective
   b. noun
   c. adjective and noun

6. I read <u>books</u>.
   a. adjective
   b. noun
   c. adjective and noun

B. Use the words in the chart to write sentences.

I am happy.   I have friends.

I	am	happy busy different
	have like	friends books information ideas

1. _____

2. _____

3. _____

4. _____

5. _____

C. Use the words in the chart to write sentences about your friends and classmates.

My friends listen.   My friends have computers.

My friends My classmates	listen talk read study	
	have	computers ideas phones

1. _____

2. _____

3. _____

4. _____

D. Write sentences. Use a capital letter and period in each sentence.

1. soccer/my friends/play

   My friends play soccer. _____

2. use/my classmates/computers

   _____

3. big/is/my school

   _____

4. like/i/my teacher

   _____

5. a small phone/have/i

   _____

Questions

A question is a type of sentence. A question begins with a capital letter and ends with a question mark (?).

capital letter   question mark   capital letter   question mark

Are you busy?   Do you like computers?

Sometimes people ask *yes/no* questions.

Questions (?)	Are you a student?	Is your classmate happy?	Do your friends play soccer?
Answers (.)	Yes, I am a student.	Yes, my classmate is happy.	Yes, my friends play soccer.
	No, I am a teacher.	No, my classmate is sad.	No, my friends read books.

Sometimes questions ask for information. These questions start with *what, where, when, who,* and *why.*

Things	What do you play?	I play soccer.
Places	Where are you?	I am at school.
Time	When do you read?	I read in the morning.
Type	What kind of books do you read?	I read interesting books.
People	Who do you like?	I like my friends.
Reason	Why are you happy?	I have many friends.

Match the questions with the answers.

1. __c__ Do you have information?

2. _____ When do you write?

3. _____ Where do you read?

4. _____ What is the book about?

5. _____ Who do you study with?

6. _____ Why do you like books?

7. _____ Is it a similar word?

8. _____ What kind of teacher do you have?

a. I write in the morning.

b. I read at school.

c. Yes, I have information.

d. The book is about English.

e. Books are interesting.

f. I study with my classmates.

g. I have an English teacher.

h. No, it is a different word.

▲▲▲ PARAGRAPHS

A paragraph explains an idea. A paragraph has a main idea sentence and three or more supporting sentences. The supporting sentences explain the main idea.

A paragraph has a title. A title tells what a paragraph is about.

Title —————

My Classroom

Indentation ————

Students are busy. Students study. Students read books. Students write.

A. Circle the correct title for each paragraph. Then circle the number of sentences in the paragraph.

1.

Words / Sentences

Sentences have words. Sentences have subjects. Sentences have verbs. Sentences use periods.

Number of sentences: 3 (4) 5

2.

My Teachers / My School

I like my school. My school has small classrooms. My school has good teachers. My school has computers.

Number of sentences: 3 4 5

3.

> # My Classmates / My Friends
>
> My classmates are interesting.
>
> My classmates ask good questions.
>
> My classmates have interesting ideas.

Number of sentences: 3   4   5

B. Read the paragraphs. Check (✓) the questions each paragraph answers.

A Happy Student

I am a happy student. I like English. I write English sentences. I use different words.

1. ○ a. What kind of student are you?

○ b. Do you like English?

○ c. What do you read?

○ d. Where do you read?

○ e. What do you write?

○ f. What do you use?

My Friends

My friends are similar. My friends like books. My friends like pictures. My friends are happy.

2. ○ a. Are your friends similar or different?

○ b. Who are your friends?

○ c. What do your friends like?

○ d. Are your friends happy or sad?

My Classroom

My classroom is big. My classroom has computers. My classroom has many books.

3. ○ a. Is your classroom big or small?

○ b. Do you like your classroom?

○ c. Does your classroom have computers?

○ d. Does your classroom have books?

○ e. Where do you study?

C. Use the titles and sentences below to write paragraphs.

1. **my friends**

   i like my friends   my friends play soccer

   my friends are happy   my friends have good ideas

   My Friends

   I like my friends. My friends are happy.

   _____

   _____

   _____

2. **my books**

   my books have interesting information   i read my books at home

   i use my books in class

   _____

   _____

   _____

   _____

   _____

3. **my classmates**

   my classmates are busy   my classmates use computers

   my classmates study English   my classmates write paragraphs

   ---

   _____

   _____

   _____

   _____

   _____

Look at the word bank for the Readiness Unit. Check (✓) the words you know.
Circle the words you want to learn better.

OXFORD 2000 🔑

Adjectives		Nouns		Verbs	
big	interesting	book	park	be	read
boring	many	classroom	phone	(am, is, are)	say
busy	new	computer	picture	explain	study
different	old	desk	question	have	use
few	red	friend	school	like	write
good	sad	idea	student	listen	
green	similar	information	teacher	play	
happy	small	morning			

PRACTICE WITH THE OXFORD 2000 🔑

A. Use the chart. Match adjectives with nouns.

1. _busy classroom_   2. _____

3. _____   4. _____

5. _____   6. _____

B. Use the chart. Match verbs with nouns.

1. _have a computer_   2. _____

3. _____   4. _____

5. _____   6. _____

C. Complete the sentences with words from the chart. Use an adjective + noun.

1. I have a ___good___ ___friend___.

2. I have a _____ _____.

3. I am a _____ _____.

4. I use a _____ _____.

5. I like my _____ _____.

6. My friend has a _____ _____.

UNIT **1** People

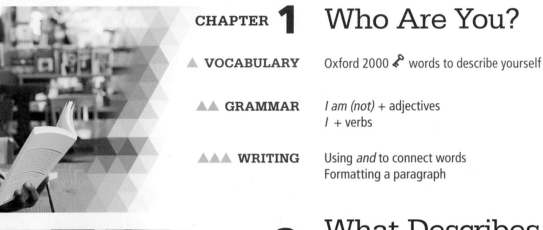

CHAPTER **1** Who Are You?

▲ **VOCABULARY**   Oxford 2000 ✎ words to describe yourself

▲▲ **GRAMMAR**   *I am (not)* + adjectives
I + verbs

▲▲▲ **WRITING**   Using *and* to connect words
Formatting a paragraph

CHAPTER **2** What Describes Your Family?

▲ **VOCABULARY**   Oxford 2000 ✎ words to describe family

▲▲ **GRAMMAR**   *we* + verbs
they + verbs

▲▲▲ **WRITING**   Using *we/our* and *they/their*
Plural nouns with *-s*

CHAPTER **3** Who Is a Good Friend?

▲ **VOCABULARY**   Oxford 2000 ✎ words to describe friends

▲▲ **GRAMMAR**   *he/she is (not)* + adjectives
he/she + verbs

▲▲▲ **WRITING**   Writing a topic sentence with an adjective
Checking for *-s* with two verbs
Using *has, goes, studies,* and *watches*

UNIT WRAP UP   Extend Your Skills

CHAPTER **1** Who Are You?

- Use *I am (not)* + adjectives
- Use *I* + verbs
- Use *and* to connect words
- Format a paragraph
- Write a paragraph about yourself

▲ VOCABULARY ▸ Oxford 2000 🔑 words to describe yourself

A. Write the correct number from the pictures next to each item in the box.

_____ travel	_____ stay home	_____ watch television	_____ visit family
_____ play games	_____ meet people	_____ use a computer	_I_ like sports

1.

2.

3.

B. Match each picture above to one of the words below.

adventurous   quiet   social

Picture 1: _____   Picture 2: _____   Picture 3: _____

C. Describe the pictures. Circle the word or words that complete the sentences.

1.

| I | *travel.* |
| | *read.* |

2.

| I am | *quiet.* |
| | *social.* |

3.

| I like | *soccer.* |
| | *computers.* |

4.

| I am | *adventurous.* |
| | *sad.* |

5.

| I | *watch television.* |
| | *read books.* |

6.

| I | *play sports.* |
| | *visit family.* |

Oxford 2000 🔑

Use the Oxford 2000 list on page 133 to find more words to describe the pictures on these pages. Share your words with a partner.

D. Circle one word to complete each sentence about you.

1. I am   *quiet.*   *social.*

2. I like   *sports.*   *television.*

3. I   *travel.*   *stay home.*

4. I play   *games.*   *sports.*

5. I meet friends at   *home.*   *school.*

GO ONLINE
for more
practice

A. Read the paragraph. Is the writer similar to you?

About Me

I am social. I like people. I meet my friends. I am not quiet. I play games. I like sports.

B. Check (✓) the picture that matches the paragraph in Activity A.

GO ONLINE
for more
practice

Grammar Note

I am (not) + adjectives

Am is a verb. Use *I am* or *I am not* with an adjective to tell about you.

      adj.   **adj.**

  I am adventurous.   *I am* social.

Use *I am not* to tell something that is not true about you.

      adj.   **adj.**

  I am not sad.   *I am not* busy.

C. Complete the sentences to tell about you. Write *I am* or *I am not*.

1. _____ busy.

2. _____ adventurous.

3. _____ quiet.

4. _____ social.

5. _____ sad.

6. _____ happy.

D. Use the words in the chart to write sentences about you.

I am happy.

I	am am not	social quiet adventurous busy sad happy interesting boring

1. _____

2. _____

3. _____

4. _____

5. _____

Grammar Note

I + verbs

Use *I* with verbs to explain what you do.

   verb   **verb**

I travel.   *I* play soccer.

Use *I* with verbs to explain what you have or like.

   verb   **verb**

I have friends.   *I* like games.

GO ONLINE
for more
practice

Grammar   23

E. Read the sentences. Fill in each blank with a verb from the box. Circle the other verbs.

travel	home	games

1. I(am)adventurous. I _____travel_____. I(meet)interesting people.

meet	computer	play

2. I like sports. I watch them on television. I _____ soccer with friends.

adventurous	travel	meet

3. I am social. I visit my friends. I _____ classmates at school.

sad	visit	quiet

4. I like books. I _____ the library. I study.

social	stay	work

5. I am busy. I go to school. I _____ .

F. Use the words to make sentences. Use a capital letter and period in each sentence.

1. meet / friends / i

I meet friends. _____

2. am / i / social

_____

3. games / play / i

_____

4. friends / i / visit

_____

5. i / quiet / not / am

_____

G. Complete each sentence. Write *am* or *have*.

1. I _____ *am* _____ not adventurous.

2. I _____ a good computer.

3. I _____ adventurous.

4. I _____ social.

5. I _____ a television.

6. I _____ a red phone.

7. I _____ not busy.

8. I _____ a big family.

H. Use the words in the chart to write sentences.

I have a computer.   I play games.

I	have	many friends a big family a small family a computer
	play like watch	games sports television
	visit	friends family neighbors

1. _____

2. _____

3. _____

4. _____

5. _____

Chant

GO ONLINE
for the
Chapter 1
Vocabulary &
Grammar Chant

Writing Assignment Write a paragraph.

Who are you?

Step 1 PREPARE

A. Read the paragraph that Sunil wrote. Are you similar or different?

> ## Busy
>
> I am busy. I study. I read. I use a computer. I play games and watch sports.

B. Answer the questions below. Use information from Sunil's paragraph.

1. What word describes Sunil? Circle the correct word.

   social   *busy*   *adventurous*

2. What questions does Sunil answer in his paragraph? Circle the correct questions.

   a. Do you stay home?

   b. Do you study?

   c. Do you read?

   d. Do you travel?

   e. Do you use a computer?

   f. Do you play games?

   g. Do you watch television?

   h. Do you watch sports?

Step 2 PREWRITE

Work with your class. Write words that go with each adjective. Use words from Sunil's paragraph to complete the first column.

I am...			
busy.	social.	adventurous.	quiet.
I... study. read.	I...	I...	I...

Step 3 WRITE

A. Answer these questions about you. Use words from your chart above.

1. What word describes you?

   I am _____.

2. What do you do? Use *I* with verbs.

   a. I _____.

   b. I _____.

   c. I _____.

   d. I _____.

Word Partners

watch television

watch sports

watch games

watch people

_____

GO ONLINE
to practice
word partners

B. Use your sentences from Activity A to write a paragraph.

_____

_____

_____

_____

_____

C. Add a title to your paragraph. _____

Step 4 REVISE

A. Read the paragraph. Are you similar or different?

Quiet

I am quiet. I stay home. I read and watch television. I use my phone and computer. I play games.

B. Read the paragraph in Activity A again. Circle _and_.

Writing Strategy

Using _and_ to connect words

Use _and_ to connect two verbs.

   I _read_.   I _travel_.   ⟶   I read **and** travel.

Use _and_ to connect two nouns.

   I visit _family_.   I visit _friends_. ⟶ I visit family **and** friends.

Use _and_ to connect two adjectives.

   I am _adventurous_.   I am _social_. ⟶ I am adventurous **and** social.

GO ONLINE
for more
practice

C. Label each underlined word. Write _V_ for verb, _A_ for adjective, or _N_ for noun. Then write a word in the blank to complete the sentence.

1. I visit my <u>friends</u> and <u>family</u>.
   $\quad$ N

2. I am <u>social</u> and _____.

3. I <u>travel</u> and _____.

4. I like my <u>teachers</u> and _____.

5. I play <u>sports</u> and _____.

6. I <u>stay</u> home and _____.

D. Read the sentences. Label each underlined word _V_ for verb, _A_ for adjective, or _N_ for noun. Then combine two of the sentences.

1. I am <u>quiet</u>. I <u>study</u>. I <u>watch</u> television.
   $\quad\quad$ A $\quad\quad$ V $\quad\quad$ V

   I am quiet. I study and watch television.

2. I have <u>friends</u>. I am <u>busy</u>. I am <u>social</u>.

   _____

3. I am <u>happy</u>. I have <u>family</u>. I have <u>friends</u>.

   _____

4. I am <u>quiet</u>. I <u>stay</u> home. I <u>read</u>.

   _____

5. I am <u>busy</u>. I am <u>adventurous</u>. I like <u>sports</u>.

   _____

6. I like my <u>friends</u>. I like my <u>family</u>. I am <u>social</u>.

   _____

✎ **E. Rewrite your paragraph from page 28. Use the questions below to help you.**

Oxford 2000 🔑

Do you need more words to write about you? Use the Oxford 2000 list on page 133 to find more words for your sentences.

Revising Questions

Can you:

- use *and* to connect words in your paragraph?
- add vocabulary words?
- add ideas?

Step 5 EDIT

Writing Strategy

Formatting a paragraph
Paragraphs have a correct format:

1 The title begins with a capital letter.

2 Paragraphs have an indent.

3 A sentence begins with a capital letter.

4 A sentence ends with a period.

5 A sentence has a space after it.

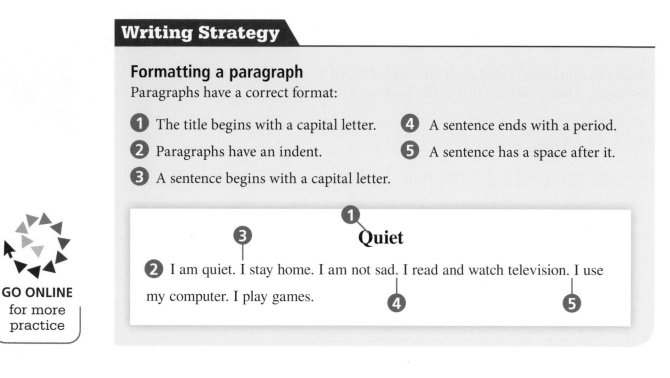

GO ONLINE for more practice

1 **Quiet**

3 **2** I am quiet. I stay home. I am not sad. I read and watch television. I use my computer. I play games. **4** **5**

A. Read the paragraph below. Find and correct four mistakes. The first mistake is corrected for you. Rewrite the corrected paragraph.

indent paragraph   **Happy**
→ I am not sad My family is big and interesting. i have friends. visit my
friends. I travel and meet people.

_____

_____

_____

_____

_____

B. Read your paragraph again. Check (✓) the things in your paragraph.

Editing Checklist

○ 1. Capital letters ○ 2. *I am not* + adjective

○ 3. Periods ○ 4. *I* + verb

○ 5. *I am* + adjective ○ 6. *and* to connect words

C. Now write your final paragraph. Use the Editing Checklist to help you.

Step 6 PUBLISH

Follow these steps to publish your paragraph.

Publishing Steps

- Share your paragraph with a partner.
- Answer the questions.
  - What word do you like in your partner's paragraph?
  - Are you similar to or different from your partner?
- Put your paragraph in your portfolio!

What Describes Your Family?

- Use *we* + verbs
- Use *they* + verbs
- Use *we/our* and *they/their*
- Use *-s* with plural nouns
- Write a paragraph about your family

▲ VOCABULARY ▸ Oxford 2000 🔑 words to describe family

A. Write the correct number from the pictures next to each item in the box.

_____ work hard	_____ parents	_1_ help neighbors	_____ sisters talk
_____ proud	_____ take care of children	_____ brothers say hello	_____ relatives eat

1.

2.

3.

B. Match each picture above to one of the words below.

polite   responsible   share food

Picture 1: _____   Picture 2: _____   Picture 3: _____

C. Write each phrase below the correct picture.

> polite neighbors ~~relatives work hard~~ sisters say hello
> proud parents responsible brother children eat food

1.

   <u>relatives work hard</u>

2.

   _____

3.

   _____

4.

   _____

5.

   _____

6.

   _____

Oxford 2000 🔑

Use the Oxford 2000 list on page 133 to find more words to describe the pictures on these pages. Share your words with a partner.

D. Write the phrases in the correct boxes in the chart.

> listen to neighbors work hard study
> ~~share food~~ say hello take care of children

Polite	Responsible
share food	

GO ONLINE
for more practice

A. Read the paragraph. Underline a sentence that also describes your family.

A Friendly Family

    I am proud of my small family. My parents and I are friendly. We help our neighbors. We say hello. We share food and talk.

B. The writer of the paragraph in Activity A has a friendly family. Circle two more words that describe the family.

quiet	polite	social

Grammar Note

we + verbs

We is a pronoun. Use *we* to describe you and one or more people. First introduce you and the people. Then use *we*.

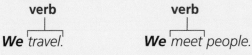

My sisters and I are happy.   **We** are happy.

Use *we are* with an adjective to tell something that is true. Use *we are not* with an adjective to tell something that is not true.

       adj.   **adj.**

We are happy.   **We are not** sad.

Use *we* with verbs to explain what you and one or more people do.

    verb   **verb**

We travel.   **We** meet people.

Use *we* with verbs to explain what you and one or more people have or like.

    verb   **verb**

We have many relatives.   **We** like our relatives.

GO ONLINE
for more
practice

C. Read the paragraph. Find three sentences where you can use *we*. Change the sentences. The first sentence is changed for you.

A Quiet Family

My family and I are quiet. ~~My family and I~~ *We* stay home. My brothers and

I read and write. My brothers and I play games. My sisters and I take care

of the house. My sisters and I help people.

D. Read the sentences. Circle the correct verbs.

1. My parents and I work hard. We   *are*   *are not*   responsible.

2. My brothers and I travel. We   *are*   *are not*   boring.

3. My relatives and I are happy. We   *are*   *are not*   sad.

4. My family and I meet people. We   *are*   *are not*   friendly.

E. Write three more sentences in each column.

Teachers	Students
1. We are busy.	1. We are busy.
2. We explain ideas.	2. We listen.
3. _____	3. _____
4. _____	4. _____
5. _____	5. _____

they + verbs

They is a pronoun. Use *they* to describe two or more people. First introduce the people. Then use *they*.

My brothers are friendly. **They** smile.

Use *they are* or *they are not* with an adjective.

They are friendly. **They are not** quiet.

Use *they* with verbs to describe what others do.

They travel. **They** meet people.

Use *they* to show what others have or like.

They have interesting children. **They** like books.

GO ONLINE
for more
practice

F. Read each sentence. Then write a sentence that explains the first sentence. Use *they* and ideas from the box.

| quiet | adventurous | social | polite | interesting | boring | busy | proud |

1. My friends work hard. _They are busy._

2. My parents share food with the neighbors. _____

3. My sisters stay home. _____

4. My neighbors travel. _____

5. Children play games. _____

6. My relatives take care of their family. _____

G. Write *we* or *they* to complete the sentences.

1. My sisters are adventurous. _They_____ travel.

2. My relatives are social. _____ have many friends.

3. My parents and I are happy. _____ play games.

4. My brothers and sisters are busy. _____ study and visit friends.

5. My friends and I are interesting. _____ read and travel.

6. My classmate and I are quiet. _____ are not social.

H. Read each sentence. Then write a sentence that gives more information using we or they.

1. My brothers and I are adventurous.

   We travel. _____

2. My parents are quiet.

   _____

3. My sisters and I are friendly.

   _____

4. My husband and I are responsible.

   _____

5. My relatives are interesting.

   _____

I. Use the words in the chart to write sentences.

We are proud.
They meet people.

We	are	proud
They	are not	polite
My parents		responsible
My brothers		adventurous
My sisters		friendly
My relatives	meet people	
	travel	
	work hard	
	share food	
	take care of children	

1. _____

2. _____

3. _____

4. _____

5. _____

Chant

GO ONLINE
for the
Chapter 2
Vocabulary &
Grammar Chant

Writing Assignment Write a paragraph.

What describes your family?

Step 1 PREPARE

A. Read the paragraph. Circle the correct title.

> ### A Responsible Family   A Friendly Family
>
> I am proud of my family. We are a responsible family. We work hard. My parents are busy. They take care of their children. My sisters and I go to school. We study. We help our parents.

B. Answer the questions about the model paragraph.

1. The writer is proud of her family. What do they do?

_____

2. What word describes the family?

_____

3. What do the parents do?

_____

4. What do the writer and sisters do?

_____

Step 2 PREWRITE

A. What adjectives describe your family? Circle the adjectives.

My family is...					
friendly	polite	responsible	interesting	adventurous	quiet
busy	happy	proud	big	small	

B. Circle words that tell what your family does.

We...		
use a computer	share food	talk
play games	work hard	visit family
like sports	help the neighbors	watch television
stay home	say hello	take care of
study		children

Step 3 WRITE

A. Answer these questions about your family.

1. Are you proud of your family?

   I am _____.

2. What word describes your family?

   My family is _____.

3. What do you do with your family?

   a. We _____.

   b. We _____.

   c. We _____.

4. What do your parents do?

   They _____.

5. What do you do with your brothers and sisters?

   We _____.

Word Partners

help children

help family

help friends

help neighbors

help people

GO ONLINE
to practice
word partners

✏ B. Use your sentences from Activity A to write a paragraph.

_____

_____

_____

_____

_____

✏ C. Add a title to your paragraph. _____

Step 4 REVISE

A. Read the paragraph. Is your family similar or different?

> # My Family
>
> I am proud of my family. My parents have many relatives. We visit their homes. They share their food. They visit our home. We eat and play with their children.

B. Read the paragraph in Activity A again. Circle *our* and *their*.

GO ONLINE
for more
practice

Writing Strategy

Using *we/our* and *they/their*
Use *our* with *we* to show ownership.

We have **neighbors.** ⟶ **Our neighbors** are friendly.

Use *their* with *they* to show ownership.

They have children. ⟶ **Their** children are polite.

C. Fill in the blanks. Use *we, our, they,* and *their.*

1. _____We_____ take care of our children.

2. They have neighbors. They like _____ neighbors.

3. We talk to _____ neighbors in the morning.

4. Our relatives share their food. _____ are friendly.

5. _____ have children. Our children are polite.

D. Read both sentences in each example. Rewrite one of the sentences so the sentences work together.

1. We have a few relatives. ~~Their~~ *Our* relatives are busy.

We have a few relatives. Our relatives are busy.

2. They have many children. Our children play games.

_____

3. We have responsible neighbors. We like their neighbors.

_____

4. My neighbors have children. We like our children.

_____

5. My brothers and I work hard. Their parents are proud.

_____

E. Unscramble the words after each sentence below to make a second sentence. Then write each new sentence. Use a capital letter and period in each sentence.

1. My brothers know about sports.
   their/share/friends/information with/they

They share information with their friends.

2. Our neighbors are responsible.
   take/they/their/children/care of

_____

3. My teachers are interesting.
   class/students/their/like/their

_____

4. I am proud of my family.
   help/and/friends/we/neighbors/our

   _____

5. They are polite.
   say/they/their/relatives/hello to

   _____

✎ **F. Rewrite your paragraph from page 40. Use the questions below to help you.**

Oxford 2000 🔑

Do you need more words to write about your family? Use the Oxford 2000 list on page 133 to find more words for your sentences.

Revising Questions

Can you:

- use *we/our* or *they/their*?

- add vocabulary words?

- add ideas?

Step 5 EDIT

GO ONLINE
for more
practice

Writing Strategy

Plural nouns with -*s*
You can add -*s* to some words to show "more than one."

one brother	two brother*s*
a sister	many sister*s*

Some words are spelled differently to show "more than one."

three children	X ~~three childs~~
two people	X ~~two persons~~

A. Read the paragraph below. Find and correct five mistakes. The first mistake is corrected for you. Rewrite the corrected paragraph.

My Family
children
  My family is big. My parents have six ~~childs~~. I have two brother. I have one sisters. My parents are proud of their childs. We work hard. We are polite. We are proud of our parents. They have many friend. They are happy.

_____

_____

_____

_____

_____

B. Read your paragraph again. Check (✓) the things in your paragraph.

Editing Checklist

○ 1. Capital letters and periods   ○ 2. *our* with *we*

○ 3. *we* + verb   ○ 4. *their* with *they*

○ 5. *they* + verb

C. Now write your final paragraph. Use the Editing Checklist to help you.

Step 6 PUBLISH

Follow these steps to publish your paragraph.

Publishing Steps

- Share your paragraph with a partner.
- Answer the questions.
  - What word do you like in your partner's paragraph?
  - Is your family similar to or different from your partner's family?
- Put your paragraph in your portfolio!

CHAPTER 3 Who Is a Good Friend?

- Use *he/she is (not)* + adjectives
- Use *he/she* + verbs
- Write a topic sentence

- Check for *-s* with two verbs
- Use *has, goes, studies,* and *watches*
- Write a paragraph about a friend

▲ VOCABULARY ► Oxford 2000 🔑 words to describe friends

A. Write the correct number from the pictures next to each item in the box.

_____ smiles   _____ eats in restaurants   _____ likes nature

_____ likes fashion   _1_ rides a bicycle   _____ has many friends

_____ intelligent   _____ takes pictures

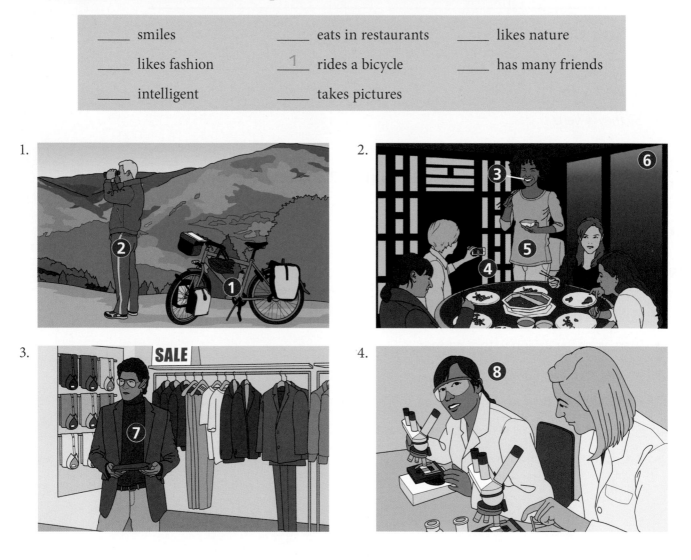

1.
2.
3.
4.

B. Match each picture above to one of the words below.

| friendly | shares ideas | active | goes shopping |

Picture 1: _____   Picture 2: _____

Picture 3: _____   Picture 4: _____

C. Write the phrases in the correct boxes in the chart.

asks polite questions   studies   rides a bicycle

eats in restaurants   likes sports   shares ideas

has many friends   reads books   smiles

Active	Intelligent	Friendly
		asks polite questions

D. Use the words in the box to complete the sentences.

share   eat   like

are   go   ride

1. My neighbors ____*are*____ active. They _____ bicycles.

2. My friends and I _____ fashion. We _____ shopping.

3. We _____ in restaurants. We _____ food.

E. Use the words in the box to complete the sentences.

is   reads   takes

likes   smiles   studies

1. Nguyen ____*likes*____ nature. He _____ pictures.

2. Salwa _____ friendly. She _____.

3. My classmate Tien is intelligent. She _____ books.
   She _____.

Oxford 2000 🔑

Use the Oxford 2000 list on page 133 to find more words to describe the pictures on page 44. Share your words with a partner.

GO ONLINE
for more practice

▲▲ GRAMMAR
▶ *he/she is (not)* + adjectives
▶ *he/she* + verbs

A. Read the paragraph about Jun and his friend. Are you similar or different?

Kurosh

Kurosh is intelligent. He likes books. He studies. He explains ideas. I am similar. We talk and share ideas.

B. Check (✓) the picture that matches the paragraph in Activity A.

Grammar Note

he/she is (not) + adjectives

Use *he is* with an adjective to tell about a male.

<u>*He is*</u> *friendly.*

Use *she is* with an adjective to tell about a female.

<u>*She is*</u> *intelligent.*

Use *he is not* to tell something that is not true about a male. Use *she is not* to tell something that is not true about a female.

He is not *sad.*

She is not *boring.*

GO ONLINE
for more practice

C. Use the words below to write sentences about the pictures.

1. he/boring

He is not boring.

2. he/intelligent

_____

3. he/happy

_____

4. she/active

_____

5. she/sad

_____

6. she/adventurous

_____

7. they/interesting

_____

8. they/boring

_____

Grammar Note

he/she + verbs

Use *I/we/they* + verb to tell about you or different people. Add an *-s* to a verb to explain what one male or one female does, likes, or has.

> I **travel**. Kenji **travels**.
> We **like** nature. Daniel **likes** nature.
> They **ride** bicycles. Salwa **rides** a bicycle.

He is a pronoun. Use *he* to describe one male. First introduce a male. Then use *he*.

> **Kenji** travels. **He** takes pictures. **He** goes shopping.

She is a pronoun. Use *she* to describe one female. First introduce a female. Then use *she*.

> **Salwa** is active. **She** rides a bicycle. **She** likes sports.

Note different spellings:

have = has	*go = goes*	*study = studies*	*watch = watches*

GO ONLINE
for more practice

D. Read each sentence. Add a second sentence that gives more information. Use the phrases in the box.

go shopping	~~have many books~~	say hello	visit my family
have many friends	play sports	study English	watch sports

1. Kurosh reads. He has many books. _____

2. Daniel watches television. _____

3. My friends and I are polite. _____

4. I travel. _____

5. Kenji is my classmate. _____

6. Salwa likes fashion. _____

7. Sophia is social. _____

8. Kurosh and Nguyen are active. _____

E. Use the words in the charts to write sentences.

My friend is active. He rides a bicycle.

My friend Nabil Sofia He She	is (not)	active boring friendly quiet intelligent
	reads books eats at restaurants has many friends goes shopping likes nature rides a bicycle stays home	

My friends are different. They take care of nature.

I	am (not)	different interesting responsible social similar
My friends We They	are (not)	
I My friends We They	like fashion smile eat with relatives go shopping take care of nature	

1. _____

2. _____

3. _____

4. _____

5. _____

6. _____

7. _____

8. _____

Chant

GO ONLINE for the Chapter 3 Vocabulary & Grammar Chant

Writing Assignment Write a paragraph.

Who is a good friend?

Step 1 PREPARE

A. Read the paragraph. Do you have a similar friend?

> ## Elsa
>
> Elsa is active. She travels. She rides a bicycle. She takes pictures. I am different. I am not active. I stay home and read books.

B. Answer the questions about the paragraph in Activity A.

1. What adjective describes Elsa?

_____

2. What does she do?

   a. _____

   b. _____

   c. _____

3. Is the writer similar or different?

_____

4. What does the writer do?

_____

Step 2 PREWRITE

A. Think about a friend. What adjectives describe your friend? Circle the adjectives.

adventurous	friendly	polite
active	quiet	happy
intelligent	busy	responsible

B. Choose one adjective that describes your friend. _____

Writing Strategy

Writing a topic sentence with an adjective

The topic sentence is often the first sentence in a paragraph. The topic sentence tells what the paragraph is mostly about.

> **Lam**
>
> topic sentence
> <u>Lam is friendly</u>. He meets people. He says hello. He helps the neighbors.

Sentences in the paragraph explain the topic sentence. The sentences explain how Lam is friendly.

GO ONLINE for more practice

C. Complete the topic sentence about your friend.

_____ is _____ .
    Name of friend   *adjective*

D. Check (✓) verbs that explain your topic sentence about your friend.

_____ stays home	_____ watches television	_____ takes pictures	_____ says hello
_____ likes fashion	_____ goes shopping	_____ plays soccer	_____ meets people
_____ likes sports	_____ plays games	_____ works hard	_____ helps people
_____ has friends	_____ takes care of children	_____ explains ideas	_____ shares food
_____ studies	_____ talks	_____ smiles	_____ travels

Step 3 WRITE

A. Answer questions about your friend.

1. What word describes your friend?

My friend is _____ .

like shopping

like restaurants

like people

like nature

like fashion

GO ONLINE
to practice
word partners

2. What does he or she do?

a. _____

b. _____

c. _____

3. Are you similar or different?

_____

4. How are you similar or different?

a. _____

b. _____

c. _____

B. Use your sentences to write a paragraph.

_____

_____

_____

_____

_____

C. Add a title to your paragraph. _____

Step 4 REVISE

A. Read the paragraph. What do you like about Sonya?

Sonya

My friend Sonya is adventurous. She travels and takes pictures. She visits friends and meets many people. I am similar. I like pictures and people.

B. Read the paragraph in Activity A again. Circle *and*.

Checking for *-s* with two verbs

Use *-s* on verbs with *he* and *she*.

verb
|
He travel**s**.

verb
|
She work**s** hard.

Use *-s* on two verbs with *and*.

verb   verb
| |
He travel**s** and meet**s** people.

verb   verb
| |
She work**s** hard and take**s** care of the children.

GO ONLINE
for more
practice

**C. Read the sentences. Underline the verbs. Then combine the sentences. Use *and*
with two verbs.**

1. He <u>uses</u> a computer. He <u>plays</u> games.

   He uses a computer and plays games.

2. She reads. She writes.

   _____

3. He smiles. He says hello.

   _____

4. She goes home. She watches television.

   _____

5. My friend travels. She meets interesting people.

   _____

D. Rewrite the paragraph. Combine the underlined sentences with *and*.

Pedro

He stays home and reads books.
Pedro is intelligent. <u>He stays home. He reads books</u>. He uses a

computer. <u>He likes information</u>. <u>He has good ideas.</u> I am similar. I study.

<u>I read books. I explain ideas.</u>

_____

_____

_____

_____

_____

✏ **E. Rewrite your paragraph from page 52. Use the questions below to help you.**

Revising Questions

Can you:

- use *and* to combine two verbs with *-s* after *he, she,* or one person?

- add vocabulary words?

- add ideas?

Step 5 EDIT

GO ONLINE
for more
practice

Writing Strategy

Using *has*, *goes*, *studies*, and *watches*
The spelling of *have, go, study,* and *watch* changes with *he* and *she*.

He **goes** shopping. ~~He gos shopping.~~
She **has** children. ~~She haves children.~~
He **studies**. ~~He studys.~~
She **watches** games. ~~She watchs games.~~

A. Read the paragraph below. Find and correct five mistakes. The first mistake is corrected for you. Rewrite the corrected paragraph.

Peishou

My friend Peishou is busy at night. He g̶o̶ *goes* home and works hard. He

studys. He writes and corrects mistakes. He uses a computer and read

information. He haves many ideas. I am different. I read book. I watch

television and play games.

_____

_____

_____

_____

_____

B. Read your paragraph again. Check (✓) the things in your paragraph.

Editing Checklist

○ 1. Capital letters

○ 3. Periods

○ 4. *is (not)* + adjective

○ 6. *he/she* + verb

○ 2. A topic sentence with an adjective (*My friend is polite.*)

○ 5. *-s* with two verbs and *and*

○ 7. *has, goes, studies,* or *watches*

C. Now write your final paragraph. Use the Editing Checklist to help you.

Step 6 PUBLISH

Follow these steps to publish your paragraph.

Publishing Steps

- Share your paragraph with a partner.
- Answer the questions.
  - What word do you like in your partner's paragraph?
  - Is your partner's friend similar to or different from your friend?
- Put your paragraph in your portfolio!

Look at the word bank for Unit 1. Check (✓) the words you know. Circle the words you want to learn better.

OXFORD 2000 🔑

Adjectives	Nouns		Verbs	
active	bicycle	neighbor	eat	take
friendly	brother	parent	go (to)	take care (of)
intelligent	child	people	help	talk
polite	computer	picture	meet	travel
proud	family	restaurant	ride	visit
quiet	fashion	shopping	share	watch
responsible	food	sister	smile	work
social	game	sport	stay	
	home	television		
	nature			

PRACTICE WITH THE OXFORD 2000 🔑

A. Use the chart. Match adjectives with nouns.

1. _____active child_____   2. _____

3. _____   4. _____

5. _____   6. _____

B. Use the chart. Match verbs with nouns.

1. _____go shopping_____   2. _____

3. _____   4. _____

5. _____   6. _____

C. Use the chart. Match verbs with adjective noun partners.

1. _meet intelligent people_   2. _____

3. _____   4. _____

5. _____   6. _____

GO ONLINE
for more
practice

UNIT **2** Geography

What Does Your Country Look Like?

- Use plural nouns
- Use *there is/there are* + nouns
- Use *there are* + *and*

- Use capital letters for names of places
- Write a paragraph about your country

▲ VOCABULARY ▸ Oxford 2000 🔑 words to describe your country

A. Write the correct number from the pictures next to each item in the box.

_____ a desert	_____ a nice beach	_____ a hotel	_____ a city
_____ a green forest	_____ a big river	_____ tall mountains	_____ tourists
_____ oceans	_1_ a beautiful lake	_____ an important building	_____ different countries

Our **Beautiful** WORLD

B. Circle the correct phrase to describe each picture.

1.

green forests
green mountains

2.

a beautiful river
a beautiful ocean

3.

red buildings
tall buildings

4.

a big lake
a small lake

5.

a nice hotel
a nice restaurant

6.

a beautiful desert
a beautiful beach

Oxford 2000 🔑

Use the Oxford 2000 list on page 133 to find more words to describe the pictures on these pages. Share your words with a partner.

C. Use the words in the box to complete the sentences.

Adjectives:	beautiful	friendly	green	old	important	nice	tall
Nouns:	beaches	forests	buildings	cities	mountains	rivers	people

1. My country has _____ _____.

2. In my country, tourists visit _____ _____.

3. My city has _____ _____.

4. I like _____ _____.

5. My friends and I visit _____ _____.

GO ONLINE
for more practice

Vocabulary   59

A. Read the paragraph. Why is South Africa beautiful?

> ## Beautiful South Africa
>
> South Africa is a beautiful country. There are two oceans. There are nice beaches. There are tall mountains and green forests. Many tourists visit Cape Town. There are important buildings and good restaurants.

B. Check (✓) the pictures that match the paragraph in Activity A.

Grammar Note

Plural nouns

You can add *-s* to a singular noun to make it plural.

a lake ➔ *two lake**s***
a river ➔ *four river**s***
a tourist ➔ *ten tourist**s***

Some plural nouns have a different spelling.

a beach ➔ *two beach**es***
a country ➔ *three countr**ies***
a city ➔ *five cit**ies***

Add -es to some nouns to make them plural. These words end with *s*, *x*, *ch*, or *sh*.

a bus → five bus**es**

a box → few box**es**

a beach → two beach**es**

a bush → many bush**es**

Some nouns end in a consonant + *y*. To make these nouns plural, drop the *y* and add -*ies*.

a country → three countr**ies**

a city → five cit**ies**

GO ONLINE
for more
practice

C. Describe each picture. Use a number with a singular or plural noun. Write *one*, *two*, *three*, or *four*.

1.

two rivers

2.

3.

4.

Dallas
Houston
San Antonio

5.

6.

SWEDEN   FINLAND
NORWAY

D. Underline the singular nouns in the sentences. Rewrite the sentences using plural nouns.

1. People see beautiful <u>mountain</u>.

People see beautiful mountains.

2. There are three important city.

_____

3. Tourist visit different country.

_____

4. They see important building.

_____

5. There are many beautiful lake and river.

_____

6. There are two ocean and many beach.

_____

GO ONLINE
for more
practice

Grammar Note

there is/there are + nouns
Use *there is* with singular nouns.

> **There is** a lake.   **There is** a restaurant.

Use *there are* with plural nouns.

> **There are** beaches.   **There are** rivers.

E. Complete each sentence. Write *there is* or *there are*.

1. There is _____ a nice hotel.

2. _____ a big desert.

3. _____ tall mountains.

4. _____ a small hotel.

5. _____ a green forest.

6. _____ a big city.

7. _____ a beautiful ocean.

8. _____ different beaches.

9. _____ nice restaurants.

10. _____ a tall building.

F. Use the map of Australia to write sentences. Use *there is* or *there are*.

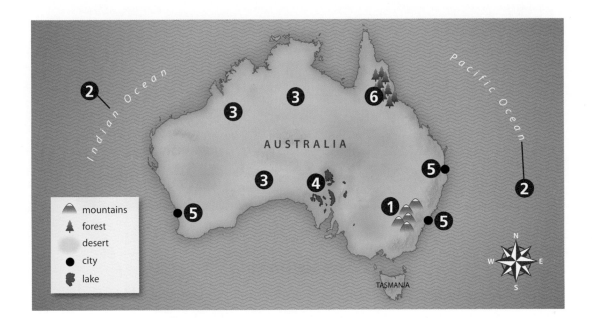

1. <u>There are mountains.</u> _____

2. _____

3. _____

4. _____

5. _____

6. _____

Chant

GO ONLINE
for the
Chapter 4
Vocabulary &
Grammar Chant

Writing Assignment Write a paragraph.

What does your country look like?

Step 1 PREPARE

A. Read Luis's paragraph. Why is Bolivia interesting?

A Visit to Bolivia

Bolivia is an interesting country. There are tall mountains and big forests. Tourists visit important cities. Many tourists like La Paz. There are beautiful buildings and nice hotels. They go shopping and eat in different restaurants.

B. Answer the questions about the model paragraph. Write sentences.

1. What country is interesting?

Bolivia is interesting.

2. Are there mountains or deserts?

_____

3. Are there small forests or big forests?

_____

4. What city do tourists like?

_____

5. What do people see in La Paz?

_____

6. What do they do?

_____

A. Circle one word that describes your country.

| beautiful | big | nice | interesting | small |

B. Complete the topic sentence about your country.

_____ is a(n) _____ country.

Name of country   adjective

C. Check (✓) what people see in your country.

_____ an ocean   _____ mountains

_____ big cities   _____ forests

_____ important buildings   _____ deserts

_____ lakes   _____ rivers

D. What city do tourists like? Check (✓) what tourists do there.

Name of city: _____

_____ eat in restaurants   _____ visit important buildings   _____ meet friendly people

_____ go shopping   _____ take pictures   _____ ride bicycles

A. Answer the questions about your country.

1. What is your country like? Is it nice, interesting, or beautiful?

_____ is a(n) _____ country.

Name of country   adjective

2. Are there mountains or forests?

There are _____.

3. Are there rivers? Are there lakes?

_____

4. What do tourists see?

_____

5. What city do tourists like? What do they do there?

_____

B. Use your sentences to write a paragraph.

_____

_____

_____

_____

_____

C. Add a title to your paragraph. _____

Word Partners

see a country

see a desert

see a river

see different places

see forests

see many cities

see mountains

GO ONLINE
to practice
word partners

Step 4 REVISE

A. Read the paragraph. What do tourists see in Canada?

Canada

Canada has beautiful nature. There are tall mountains and big lakes. There are tall green trees. There are many rivers and two oceans. Many tourists visit Canada. They take many beautiful pictures.

B. Read the paragraph in Activity A again. Circle *and*.

Writing Strategy

Using *there are* + *and*
Use *there are* with plural nouns. Use *and* with two plural nouns.

There are restaurants. There are hotels. ⟶ There are restaurants **and** hotels.

There are beautiful lakes. There are rivers. ⟶ There are beautiful lakes **and** rivers.

GO ONLINE for more practice

C. Use the words to write sentences. Use *there are* with *and* in your sentences.

1. rivers, lakes _There are rivers and lakes._ _____

2. mountains, forests _____

3. hotels, restaurants _____

4. two oceans, many beaches _____

5. interesting cities, tall buildings _____

6. beautiful mountains, big rivers _____

D. Use *there are* with two nouns. Use *and*. Write the paragraph in your notebook.

> There are beautiful cities and interesting buildings.
> Australia is a nice country. ~~There are beautiful cities. There are interesting buildings.~~ Many tourists like Melbourne. There are good restaurants. There are nice hotels. Tourists visit different places. There are old buildings. There are new buildings.

E. Rewrite your paragraph from page 66. Use the questions below to help you.

Revising Questions

Can you:

- use *there are* with *and* to combine nouns in your paragraph?

- add vocabulary words?

- add ideas?

Oxford 2000 🔑

Do you need more words to write about your country? Use the Oxford 2000 list on page 133 to find more words for your sentences.

Writing Strategy

Capital letters for names of places
Use a capital letter for the names of countries and cities.

> _South Africa is a beautiful country. [name of country]_
>
> _Tourists visit Cape Town. [name of city]_
>
> _Tourists like Sydney, Australia. [name of city, name of country]_

Use a capital letter for proper nouns. Do not use a capital letter for common nouns.

> _Bolivia is interesting. [proper noun]_
>
> _My country is interesting. [common noun]_
>
> _Tourists visit La Paz. [proper noun]_
>
> _Tourists visit interesting cities. [common noun]_

GO ONLINE
for more
practice

A. Read the sentences. Use a capital letter with proper nouns. Use the map to help you.

1. There are many beaches in ~~t~~hailand.

2. Tourists like to visit bangkok and eat in good restaurants.

3. There are two important cities in vietnam. They are hanoi and ho chi minh city.

4. Many people visit phnom penh, cambodia. They see important buildings.

5. I like malaysia. It is a beautiful country.

6. There are tall buildings in kuala lumpur.

B. Read the paragraph below. Find and correct eight mistakes. The first mistake is corrected for you.

Visiting Australia

Many tourists like australia. There are many important city. Tourist

visit sydney. They see interesting buildings. They eat at nice restaurant.

Tourists like brisbane, australia. They visit beautiful forests and park.

C. Read your paragraph again. Check (✓) the things in your paragraph.

Editing Checklist

○ 1. Capital letters
○ 2. *there is* + singular nouns
○ 3. Periods
○ 4. *there are* + plural nouns
○ 5. *-s, -es, -ies* with plural nouns
○ 6. *there are* + *and*

D. Now write your final paragraph. Use the Editing Checklist to help you.

Step 6 PUBLISH

Follow these steps to publish your paragraph.

Publishing Steps

• Share your paragraph with a partner.

• Answer the questions.

  • What word do you like in your partner's paragraph?

  • What place do you want to visit?

• Put your paragraph in your portfolio!

CHAPTER 5

What Is Your Favorite City?

- Use *a/an* + singular count nouns
- Use the pronouns *it* and *they*
- Use simple sentences with *and*
- Use prepositional phrases at the end of a sentence
- Write a paragraph about your favorite city

▲ VOCABULARY ▶ Oxford 2000 🔑 words to describe your favorite city

A. Write the correct number from the pictures next to each item in the box.

_____ a market	_____ my favorite city	_1_ crowded streets	_____ walk at night
_____ a modern subway	_____ shop at famous stores	_____ watch people on the street	_____ wear fashionable clothes
_____ drink coffee at a café	_____ buy fresh seafood	_____ play music	

B. Write each sentence below the correct picture.

| Musicians play music at night. | I read a book on a quiet street. |
| She buys old clothes. | There is a crowded subway. |

1. _____

2. _____

3. _____

4. _____

Oxford 2000 🔑

Use the Oxford 2000 list on page 133 to find more words to describe the pictures on these pages. Share your words with a partner.

C. Use the words in the box to complete the sentences.

| Adjectives: | beautiful | crowded | famous | interesting | old | | modern |
| Nouns: | buildings | cafés | clothes | markets | restaurants | stores |

1. My city has _____ _____.

2. In my city, tourists visit _____ _____.

3. My neighborhood has _____ _____.

4. I take pictures of _____ _____.

5. People wear _____ _____.

GO ONLINE
for more practice

▲▲ GRAMMAR
▶ *a/an* + singular count nouns
▶ Pronouns *it* and *they*

A. Read the paragraph. Where is Yokohama?

An Interesting City

Yokohama is my favorite city. It is an interesting city in Japan. It is near the ocean. Yokohama has a modern subway and tall buildings. I walk on crowded streets and buy clothes at famous stores.

B. Read the sentences below. Check (✓) sentences that are true about the paragraph in Activity A.

_____ 1. There is a modern subway.

_____ 2. There are tall buildings.

_____ 3. Yokohama is boring.

_____ 4. There are many people.

_____ 5. Yokohama is a quiet city.

Grammar Note

a/an + singular count nouns

Use *a* or *an* before a singular count noun.

Use *a* or *an* before an adjective + singular count noun.

Use *an* before a word that begins with *a, e, i, o,* and sometimes *u.*

an   *idea*

an ocean   **an** active student   **an** interesting store   **an** old building

Use *a* before words that begin with other letters.

a   *restaurant*

a city   **a** hotel   **a** quiet street   **a** tall building   **a** modern subway

GO ONLINE
for more
practice

C. Write *a* or *an*.

1. __a__ subway

2. _____ market

3. _____ ocean

4. _____ interesting building

5. _____ fashionable store

6. _____ old café

7. _____ building

8. _____ country

9. _____ idea

10. _____ modern city

D. Complete the sentences about Yokohama. Use *a*, *an*, or *many*.

1. Yokohama has _____a_____ river.

2. It has _____ famous stores.

3. There are _____ tall buildings.

4. Yokohama is _____ old city.

5. It has _____ crowded streets.

6. There is _____ good subway.

7. It has _____ interesting seafood market.

8. Yokohama is _____ nice place for shopping.

9. People play _____ sports.

10. Visitors can see _____ famous garden.

Grammar Note

Pronouns *it* and *they*

It and *they* are pronouns. A pronoun is a word that replaces a noun.

It can be used in place of a singular noun.

*I walk to a **café** in the morning. **It** has good coffee.*

They can be used in place of a plural noun.

*There are many famous **stores**. **They** have nice clothes.*

First introduce a noun. Then use the pronoun.

*I like **Yokohama**. **Yokohama** is an interesting city. **Yokohama** has a modern subway and glass skyscrapers.*	→ *I like **Yokohama**. **It** is an interesting city. **It** has a modern subway and glass skyscrapers.*
***The city streets** are interesting. **The city streets** have restaurants and stores. **The city streets** are busy at night.*	→ ***The city streets** are interesting. **They** have restaurants and stores. **They** are busy at night.*

GO ONLINE
for more
practice

E. Write the sentences. Replace the underlined words with *it* or *they*.

1. Cape Town is a beautiful city. <u>Cape Town</u> has many green trees.

   <u>Cape Town is a beautiful city. It has many green trees.</u>

2. We listen to musicians. <u>Musicians</u> play good music.

   _____

3. New York is a big city. <u>New York</u> has many people.

   _____

4. Yokohama has glass skyscrapers. <u>Glass skyscrapers</u> are tall and modern.

_____

5. Many tourists visit New York. <u>Many tourists</u> buy clothes at famous stores.

_____

6. I see a busy café. <u>A busy café</u> is crowded.

_____

7. I like my city. <u>My city</u> has many different people. <u>Many different people</u> have interesting ideas.

_____

8. We walk on city streets. <u>City streets</u> are interesting.

_____

9. My friends drink coffee. <u>Coffee</u> is a popular drink.

_____

10. The markets sell fruit. <u>The markets</u> also sell flowers.

_____

F. Read each sentence. Write a second sentence with _it_ or _they_. Draw an arrow to the noun _it_ or _they_ replaces.

1. My city has many buildings. They are tall. _____

2. My classmates like this book. _____ _____

3. My parents go to a good market. _____

4. There are three cafés on this street. _____

5. My friends have a favorite park. _____

6. My parents live near a mountain. _____

7. The city has a new library. _____

8. We play sports at the school. _____

Writing Assignment Write a paragraph.

What is your favorite city?

Step 1 PREPARE

A. Read Carmen's paragraph. Is Boston interesting?

> ## Boston
>
> I am proud of my city. My friends and I go out at night. We see musicians on the street and listen to good music. I go to a famous market in the morning and buy fresh seafood. I see many interesting people.

B. Answer the questions about the model paragraph. Write sentences.

1. What does Carmen do at night?

_____

2. What does she see? What does she listen to?

_____

3. Where does Carmen go in the morning? What does she do?

_____

Step 2 PREWRITE

A. Write the names of cities that match the descriptions below. Talk about them. Circle one to write about.

a big, busy city

_____

a quiet city

_____

a city by the ocean

_____

a city in the mountains

_____

a modern city

_____

an old city

_____

B. Complete the topic sentence about your favorite city.

_____ is my favorite city.

C. Check (✓) what your favorite city has.

1. _____ a market   2. _____ streets

3. _____ a subway   4. _____ stores

5. _____ cafés   6. _____ buildings

D. Write what you do and see in your favorite city.

What I do	What I see
eat in restaurants	old buildings

Step 3 WRITE

A. Answer the questions about your favorite city. Write sentences using words from your chart.

1. What is your favorite city?

My favorite city is _____.

2. Is it interesting, modern, or old?

_____

3. What does it have?

_____

4. What do you do there?

_____

5. What do you see?

_____

6. What do you listen to?

_____

Word Partners

famous city

famous places

famous people

famous restaurants

famous stores

GO ONLINE
to practice
word partners
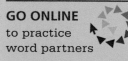

B. Use your sentences to write a paragraph.

_____

_____

_____

_____

_____

C. Add a title to your paragraph. _____

Step 4 REVISE

A. Read the paragraph. Why is London interesting?

London

I like London. It has people from different countries. They wear fashionable clothes. They meet at many cafés and share interesting ideas. I listen to people and have fresh ideas.

B. Read the paragraph in Activity A again. Circle *and*.

Writing Strategy

Simple sentences with *and*
A simple sentence has one subject and one or more verbs.

subject   *verb*

London is an interesting city.

subject   *verb*   *verb*

People meet at cafés and share interesting ideas.

Use a simple sentence with *and* to combine sentences with the same subject.

I walk on crowded streets.   *I shop in famous stores.*

I walk on crowded streets and shop in famous stores.

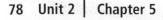

GO ONLINE
for more
practice

C. Read the sentences. Use *and* to combine two sentences with the same subject.

1. Boston is an old city. There are many parks. People walk on interesting streets. They drink coffee at cafés.

   People walk on interesting streets and drink coffee at cafés.

2. I like Houston. It has nature. People ride bicycles. They meet at parks.

   _____

3. The restaurants are good in Dubai. Tourists listen to nice music. Tourists eat good food.

   _____

4. Esfahan is friendly. People walk to stores. They talk to neighbors. The streets are busy at night.

   _____

5. Vancouver is by the ocean. People sit by the water. People watch the water.

   _____

D. Complete the sentences.

1. Families meet at the park and _____.

2. Tourists go to restaurants and _____.

3. Students walk to coffee shops and _____.

4. People ride the subway and _____.

5. Children see their friends and _____.

E. Rewrite your paragraph from page 78. Use the questions below to help you.

Revising Questions

Can you:

- use simple sentences with *and*?

- add vocabulary words?

- add ideas?

Oxford 2000 🔑

Do you need more words to write about your favorite city? Use the Oxford 2000 list on page 133 to find more words for your sentences.

Writing Strategy

Prepositional phrases at the end of a sentence

You can add a prepositional phrase to the end of a sentence to give more information. Prepositional phrases often tell where or when something happens.

A prepositional phrase begins with a preposition, such as *on, at, by, to,* or *in.*

prepositional phrase

*I walk **on crowded streets**.*

preposition

<table>
<tr><th>Where</th><th>When</th></tr>
<tr><td>We drink coffee at a café.
Musicians play on the street.</td><td>I drink coffee in the morning.
They play music at night.</td></tr>
</table>

GO ONLINE
for more
practice

A. Underline the prepositional phrases in the paragraph.

I like my neighborhood <u>in Seattle</u>. I walk to school and look at the nice houses. I meet my friends in the afternoon. We drink coffee at a café. We watch people on the street.

B. Add prepositional phrases from the box to the sentences that follow.

When	Where	
in the morning in the afternoon at night	at school at home at a café	on the street by the water at a park

1. I watch people <u>on the street</u> _____.

2. We go shopping _____.

3. I work _____.

4. My friends and I talk _____.

5. My family and I stay home _____.

6. We eat _____.

C. Read the paragraph below. Find and correct eight mistakes. The first mistake is corrected for you.

indent paragraph
→

An Old City

I love in the morning Budapest. I visit a old café drink coffee. I read good book. I watch on the street people. They buy at famous stores clothes. They meet friends

D. Read your paragraph again. Check (✓) the things in your paragraph.

Editing Checklist

○ 1. Capital letters   ○ 2. *it* or *they*

○ 3. Periods   ○ 4. Simple sentences with *and*

○ 5. *a/an* + singular count nouns   ○ 6. Prepositional phrases

E. Now write your final paragraph. Use the Editing Checklist to help you.

Step 6 PUBLISH

Follow these steps to publish your paragraph.

Publishing Steps

- Share your paragraph with a partner.
- Answer the questions.
    - What do you like in your partner's paragraph?
    - Did you learn something new? What?
- Put your paragraph in your portfolio!

- Use *always, often, never* with verbs
- Use count and noncount nouns
- Use compound sentences with *and*
- Use *and* to combine supporting sentences
- Write a paragraph about a good traveler

▲ **VOCABULARY** ▶ Oxford 2000 🔑 words to describe a good traveler

A. Write the correct number from the pictures next to each item in the box.

____ brings a camera, gets lost in nature	____ tries new food, spends money
____ a careful shopper, complains about prices	____ forgets some things
_1_ organized travelers, make travel plans	____ uses a map, wears comfortable clothes, finds historic neighborhoods

B. Write each phrase below the correct picture.

forgets money	a historic building
a new camera	eat interesting food

1.

forgets money

2.

3.

4.

Oxford 2000 🔑

Use the Oxford 2000 list on page 133 to find more words to describe the pictures on these pages. Share your words with a partner.

C. Complete the sentences about Salou.

1. Salou   *brings   spends*   travel books.

2. Salou   *plans   tries*   interesting food.

3. Salou   *finds   brings*   new restaurants.

4. Salou   *makes   spends*   travel plans.

5. Salou   *meets   sees*   historic places.

6. Salou   *uses   forgets*   a map on his phone.

7. Salou   *wears   complains*   about crowded subways.

8. Salou   *tries   spends*   money.

GO ONLINE
for more
practice

▲▲ GRAMMAR
▶ *always, often, never* with verbs
▶ Count and noncount nouns

A. Read the paragraph. Are you an organized traveler?

An Organized Traveler

My brother is an organized traveler. He always brings a lot of books. He reads about cities and historic neighborhoods. He uses a map, and he never gets lost. He often brings a camera. He finds interesting places and takes pictures of famous buildings. He sees different cities, and he is happy.

B. Check (✓) the picture that matches the paragraph in Activity A.

Grammar Note

always, often, never with verbs

Always, *often*, and *never* are adverbs of frequency. Adverbs give more information about a verb. Adverbs often come before a verb in a sentence.

    adverb   verb

He **always brings** a lot of books.

When is it true?	Adverb of frequency	Sentence
100% of the time	*always*	I **always** bring a book.
50–70% of the time	*often*	I **often** take pictures.
0% of the time	*never*	She **never** sleeps late.

GO ONLINE
for more
practice

C. **Read the paragraph in Activity A again. Find each adverb and the verb it describes. Underline each adverb. Draw a circle around each verb.**

D. **Complete each sentence with *always, often,* or *never*. There may be more than one correct adverb.**

1. My parents are adventurous people. They _____ always _____ visit new places.

2. My friend is organized. She _____ makes good travel plans.

3. I _____ see my friends. I am social.

4. He is a polite traveler. He _____ complains about the food.

5. I like good food. I _____ go to restaurants.

6. She is a fashionable person. She _____ goes shopping.

7. They use a map. They _____ get lost.

E. **Rewrite each sentence. Add *always, often,* or *never* to the sentence.**

1. My teacher gives homework.

My teacher often gives homework.

2. I forget my books for class.

_____

3. I study with friends.

_____

4. My mother tries new food.

_____

5. My friends and I take pictures at school.

_____

6. My father complains about prices.

_____

7. Organized travelers use maps.

_____

Grammar Note

Count and noncount nouns

Count nouns have a number. They can be singular or plural.

Singular count nouns:	*a camera*	*a map*	*one trip*
Plural count nouns:	*cameras*	*two maps*	*many trips*

Count nouns can use singular or plural verbs.

Singular verb:	*A city **has** crowded streets.*
Plural verb:	*Cities **have** many restaurants.*

Noncount nouns do not have a number. They are never plural.

Noncount nouns: *coffee   fashion   food   information   money   music   nature   photography   seafood*

Noncount nouns use a singular verb.

*There **is** music at night.*

*Nature **has** tall mountains and green forests.*

GO ONLINE
for more
practice

F. Read the paragraph below. Look at the underlined nouns. Write the singular and plural nouns in the chart.

I am a careful <u>traveler</u>, and I always make a travel <u>plan</u>. I bring comfortable <u>clothes</u>. I read <u>books</u>, and I talk to <u>friends</u>. I use a <u>map</u> on my <u>phone</u> and find important <u>places</u> to visit. I never forget my <u>camera</u>. I visit historic <u>buildings</u>, and I take a lot of beautiful <u>pictures</u>.

Singular nouns	Plural nouns
traveler	

G. Read the paragraph below. Look at the underlined nouns. Write the count and noncount nouns in the chart.

Many <u>tourists</u> visit my <u>city</u>. Tourists often drink <u>coffee</u> at <u>cafés</u> and watch people. They see interesting <u>fashion</u>. They have new <u>ideas</u> and spend <u>money</u> at different <u>stores</u>. At night they eat in <u>restaurants</u>. They try new <u>food</u> and listen to good <u>music</u>. They smile, and they are friendly.

Count nouns	Noncount nouns
tourists	

H. Use *there is* or *there are* to complete each sentence.

1. ___There are___ tourists.

2. _____ a bridge.

3. _____ bicycles.

4. _____ historic buildings.

5. _____ interesting information.

6. _____ money.

I. Use the words in the chart to write sentences about how you travel.

I use a map.

| I | bring
use | a camera
a computer
a map
a phone |
| | | food
information
money |

1. _____

2. _____

3. _____

4. _____

Chant

GO ONLINE
for the
Chapter 6
Vocabulary &
Grammar Chant

Writing Assignment Write a paragraph.

Who is a good traveler?

Step 1 PREPARE

A. Read the paragraph about Kenji. Do you know someone like Kenji?

An Adventurous Traveler

Kenji is an adventurous traveler. He never uses a map, and he always finds interesting places. He sees a lot of nature. He visits beautiful mountains and oceans. He often goes to cities. He never goes to famous stores. He rides his bicycle and walks on historic streets.

B. Which sentences are true about Kenji? Circle two.

a. Kenji is active.   b. Kenji complains.   c. Kenji likes nature.

C. Answer the questions about the paragraph about Kenji.

1. What kind of traveler is Kenji? _Kenji is an adventurous traveler._

2. What does he see? _____

3. What does he do? _____

4. What does he never do? _____

Step 2 PREWRITE

A. Work with a partner. Write words and phrases that describe each type of traveler.

Likes cities	Likes nature
famous restaurants	tall mountains

B. Choose a good traveler to write about. Does your traveler like cities or nature? Underline words in the chart on page 88 that tell about your traveler. Write the name of your traveler below.

Name: _____

C. Complete the topic sentence about your traveler. What kind of traveler is he or she?

_____ is a(n) _____ traveler.
       Name   *adjective*

Step 3 WRITE

A. Answer these questions about your traveler. Write sentences. Use the chart on page 88 to help you.

1. What kind of traveler is he or she?

_____

2. What does he or she bring?

_____

3. What places does he or she visit?

   a. _____

   b. _____

4. What does he or she always, often, or never do?

_____

B. Use your sentences to write a paragraph.

_____

_____

_____

_____

_____

C. Add a title to your paragraph. _____

Word Partners

bring (my) family

bring a friend

bring food

bring a map

bring money

GO ONLINE
to practice
word partners

A. Read the paragraph. How is Loretta different from Kenji?

An Interesting Traveler

Loretta is an interesting traveler. She wears fashionable clothes and eats in many good restaurants. She likes shopping, and she always brings a lot of money. She visits crowded streets with famous stores, and she likes restaurants with fresh seafood. She never complains about prices.

B. Read the paragraph in Activity A again. Circle *and*.

Writing Strategy

Compound sentences with *and*

A simple sentence has one subject and one or more verbs.

   subject verb

Loretta is an interesting traveler.

     subject   verb   **verb**

Loretta wears fashionable clothes and eats in many good restaurants.

A compound sentence combines two sentences with *and*. It has two subject-verb combinations. Use a comma before *and*.

Sentence 1: *Loretta is an interesting traveler.*

Sentence 2: *She visits different cities.*

  subject + verb   **subject + verb**

Loretta is an interesting traveler, **and** *she visits different cities.*

Sentence 1: *Loretta likes shopping.*

Sentence 2: *Kenji likes historic neighborhoods.*

  subject + verb   **subject + verb**

Loretta likes shopping, **and** *Kenji likes historic neighborhoods.*

GO ONLINE
for more
practice

C. Read each sentence. Label the sentence *S* (simple sentence) or *C* (compound sentence).

_S_ 1. I see new places and meet new friends.

_C_ 2. I like shopping, and I find interesting markets.

_____ 3. My father uses a map, and we never get lost.

_____ 4. He sees different cities.

_____ 5. Lubna is a careful and polite traveler, and people help her.

_____ 6. She often complains about prices.

_____ 7. My friend likes new restaurants and often tries new food.

D. Answer the two questions in one sentence. Use a compound sentence with a comma + *and*.

1. What do organized travelers do, and what do they use?

They make travel plans, and they use a map.

2. Where do travelers stay, and where do they eat?

_____

3. When are cafés crowded, and what do people do there?

_____

4. What places do you often visit, and what places do your parents visit?

_____

5. What do careful travelers do, and what do they never do?

_____

E. Rewrite your paragraph from page 89. Use the questions below to help you.

Revising Questions

Can you:

- use compound sentences with *and*?
- add vocabulary words?
- add ideas?

Oxford 2000 🔑

Do you need more words to write about your good traveler? Use the Oxford 2000 list on page 133 to find more words for your sentences.

Writing Strategy

Using *and* to combine supporting sentences

A topic sentence tells about a topic. A supporting sentence explains the writer's meaning.

| topic sentence | supporting sentences |

Layla loves shopping. She goes to famous stores. She buys beautiful clothes.

Use a simple sentence or a compound sentence to combine two supporting sentences about the same subject.

simple sentence with one subject and two verbs

*Layla loves shopping. **She** goes to famous stores and buys beautiful clothes.*

compound sentence

*Layla loves shopping. **She** goes to stores, and **her friends** often go with her.*

Use a compound sentence to combine two supporting sentences with different subjects.

*Jorge likes restaurants. **He** meets his friends, and **they** eat together.*

*My classmates and I are different. **They** like soccer, and **I** like fashion.*

GO ONLINE
for more
practice

A. Read the sentences below. Underline the topic sentence. Combine the two supporting detail sentences with *and*. Use a simple or compound sentence.

1. <u>Fiona likes people.</u> She travels with friends. They always have fun.

   She travels with friends, and they always have fun.

2. My teacher is a social traveler. She meets many people. They tell her about their country.

   _____

3. Tien is an organized traveler. He reads travel books. He makes good travel plans.

   _____

4. Enrique is a responsible traveler. He is polite. People like him.

   _____

5. My mother is adventurous. She travels to different countries. She tries new food.

   _____

B. Read the paragraph below. Find and correct seven mistakes. The first mistake is corrected for you.

A Busy Traveler

Othman is a busy traveler. He is a soccer player*comma*, and he takes a lot of trips. He travels with his team, and plays a lot of games. He sees a lot of cities. He goes to restaurants and he tries food new. He meets often people, and They ask questions. Never he has time to see places.

C. Read your paragraph again. Check (✓) the things in your paragraph.

Editing Checklist

○ 1. Capital letters   ○ 2. Noncount nouns

○ 3. Periods   ○ 4. Compound sentences with *and*

○ 5. *always, often, never* before verbs   ○ 6. *and* to combine two supporting sentences

D. Now write your final paragraph. Use the Editing Checklist to help you.

Step 6 PUBLISH

Follow these steps to publish your paragraph.

Publishing Steps

• Share your paragraph with a partner.

• Answer the questions.

　• What word do you like in your partner's paragraph?

　• Are you similar to or different from the traveler in the paragraph?

• Put your paragraph in your portfolio!

Look at the word bank for Unit 2. Check (✓) the words you know. Circle the words you want to learn better.

OXFORD 2000 ⚷

Adjectives	Nouns			Verbs
beautiful	beach	lake	plan	bring
careful	building	map	price	buy
crowded	camera	market	river	complain
famous	city	money	seafood	drink
fashionable	clothes	mountain	shopper	find
favorite	coffee	music	store	forget
fresh	country	musician	street	get
historic	desert	nature	thing	make
important	food	night	tourist	plan
lost	forest	ocean	traveler	see
modern	hotel	place	trip	spend
nice				try
organized				walk
some				wear
tall				

PRACTICE WITH THE OXFORD 2000 ⚷

A. Use the chart. Match adjectives with nouns.

1. _____beautiful forest_____   2. _____

3. _____   4. _____

5. _____   6. _____

B. Use the chart. Match verbs with nouns.

1. _____spend money_____   2. _____

3. _____   4. _____

5. _____   6. _____

C. Use the chart. Match verbs with adjective noun partners.

1. _wear fashionable clothes_   2. _____

3. _____   4. _____

5. _____   6. _____

GO ONLINE
for more
practice

UNIT 3 Money

- Use *does not* + verbs
- Use verbs + *about*
- Use compound sentences with *but*
- Use *for example*
- Write a paragraph about someone who gets a good deal

▲ VOCABULARY ▶ Oxford 2000 ⚿ words to describe a good deal

A. Write the correct number from the pictures next to each item in the box.

_____ saves money on clothes	_____ buys jewelry online	_____ cheap shoes
_____ learns about fashion	_____ shops in stores, buys new products	_____ expensive shoes
_____ knows a lot about electronics	_____ gives advice about technology	_____ does not pay full price, gets a good deal
__1__ compares prices		

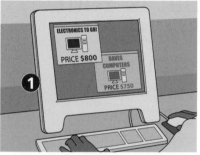

B. Circle the words that describe the pictures.

1.

   compare prices

   compare electronics

2.

   a blue phone

   an expensive phone

3.

   get a good deal

   pay full price

4.

   shop online

   shop in stores

Oxford 2000 🔑

Use the Oxford 2000 list on page 133 to find more words to describe the pictures on these pages. Share your words with a partner.

C. Write the phrases in the correct boxes in the chart.

compares prices	forgets money	saves money	pays full price
gives bad shopping advice	learns about products	knows about good deals	spends a lot of money

An intelligent shopper always...	An intelligent shopper never...
compares prices	gives bad shopping advice

GO ONLINE for more practice

A. Read the paragraph. Is Phuong an intelligent shopper?

A Fashionable Girl

Phuong knows a lot about clothes. She likes fashion. She gives good advice about shopping, and she knows about prices. For example, she buys expensive shoes, but she does not pay full price. She shops in stores, and she finds good deals. She always looks beautiful, but she does not spend a lot of money.

B. Read the paragraph in Activity A again. Circle the correct answers.

1. Phuong   (likes)   does not like   clothes.

2. She   learns   does not learn   about prices.

3. She   buys   does not buy   cheap shoes.

4. She   shops   does not shop   online.

5. She   gets   does not get   bad deals.

6. She   saves   does not save   money.

Grammar Note

does not + verbs

Use *does not* + a verb to tell when something is not true.

Use *does not* + a verb after *he*.
  He spends money on expensive clothes. He **does not buy** cheap clothes.

Use *does not* + a verb after *she*.
  She saves money. She **does not pay** full price.

Use *does not* + verb after *it* and other singular nouns.
  My city is old. It **does not have** a modern subway.

GO ONLINE for more practice

C. Read each topic sentence. Circle the two correct supporting sentences.

1. **Topic Sentence:** My brother always pays full price for electronics.

   a. He does not get good deals.

   b. He does not like new technology.

   c. He does not save money.

2. **Topic Sentence:** Petra is not a careful shopper.

    a. She does not compare prices.

    b. She does not learn about products.

    c. She does not spend a lot of money.

3. **Topic Sentence:** Lubna buys cheap jewelry online.

    a. She does not know about prices.

    b. She does not spend a lot of money.

    c. She does not shop in stores.

4. **Topic Sentence:** Ian knows a lot about electronics.

    a. He reads about new technology.

    b. He does not compare products.

    c. He learns about phones and computers.

5. **Topic Sentence**: My city is small and quiet.

    a. It does not have jewelry stores.

    b. It does not have many people.

    c. It does not have crowded streets.

D. Mrs. Loya is an English teacher. Read the topic sentence. Then write supporting sentences about Mrs. Loya. Use *does not* + verb.

Topic Sentence: Mrs. Loya is a good English teacher.

1. she/forget names

She does not forget names. _____

2. she/complain about students

_____

3. she/give bad advice

_____

4. she/have boring classes

_____

5. she/use her phone in class

_____

Grammar Note

Verbs + *about*

Many verbs are followed by prepositions. These verbs are often paired with *about* + a noun.

complain about: She does not **complain about** noun money.

know about: My friend **knows about** noun electronics.

learn about: He **learns about** new noun computers.

read about: I **read about** new noun products.

give advice about: The store **gives advice about** noun computers.

talk about: Customers **talk about** good noun prices.

write about: Students **write about** interesting noun ideas.

GO ONLINE
for more
practice

E. Answer the questions. Write sentences.

1. What do careful shoppers read about?

Careful shoppers read about products.

2. What do musicians write about?

_____

3. What do customers never complain about?

_____

4. What does a fashionable person know about?

_____

5. What do good parents give advice about?

_____

6. What do your friends talk about?

_____

F. Use the words in the charts to write sentences.

I often read about soccer.

My parents always talk about sports.

I My friends My parents	always often never	complain know learn read give advice talk write	about	clothes electronics music people prices soccer sports

An intelligent shopper knows about good deals.

He does not buy expensive products.

A careful shopper An intelligent shopper He She	knows a lot about	cheap prices different products good deals new products similar stores
	does not	buy expensive products forget about prices get bad deals pay full price spend a lot of money

1. _____

2. _____

3. _____

4. _____

5. _____

6. _____

Chant

GO ONLINE
for the
Chapter 7
Vocabulary &
Grammar Chant

Writing Assignment Write a paragraph.

Who gets a good deal?

Step 1 **PREPARE**

A. Read the paragraph about Mehmet. Are you and Mehmet similar or different?

Smart Mehmet

My friend Mehmet is intelligent, and he knows a lot about computers. He has four computers in his house. He reads about technology online, and he learns about new products. He usually gets good deals on new computers. For example, he compares prices online, and he does not pay full price. He buys new technology, but he always saves money.

B. Answer the questions about the model paragraph. Write sentences.

1. What does Mehmet know about?

_____

2. How does he learn about new technology?

_____

3. How does he get a good deal?

_____

4. What does he not do?

_____

Step 2 **PREWRITE**

A. Think about a friend, a classmate, and a relative. Write each person's name. Then choose a product that he or she knows a lot about.

electronics	clothes	phones
computers	jewelry	shoes

	Name	Product
1. A friend		
2. A classmate		
3. A relative		

B. Choose one friend, classmate, or relative to write about. Complete the topic sentence.

_____ knows a lot about _____ .
Name of person   *product*

C. Think about how the person shops. What does he or she do? What does he or she not do?

What he or she does	What he or she does not do
compares prices	pay full price

Step 3 WRITE

A. Answer the questions about the person for your paragraph. Write sentences using words from the chart above.

1. Is the person your friend, classmate, or relative? What does he or she know a lot about?

_____

2. How does he or she learn about products?

_____

3. What does he or she buy?

_____

4. Where does he or she shop?

_____

Word Partners

get a few things

get a good deal

get a computer

get money

get information

_____

GO ONLINE
to practice
word partners

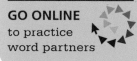

Writing   103

5. How does he or she get a good deal?

_____

6. What does he or she not do?

_____

✍ **B. Use your sentences to write a paragraph in your notebook.**

✍ **C. Add a title to your paragraph.** _____

Step 4 **REVISE**

A. Read the paragraph. Where does Lubna shop?

> ## Lubna's Jewelry
>
> My sister Lubna buys and sells jewelry. She works hard, but she makes a lot of money. She visits famous stores and gets a lot of information about products. For example, she talks to people and asks many questions. She buys a lot of jewelry, but she does not pay full price. She puts pictures of her products online, and customers buy her jewelry. Her customers get a good deal, and she often gives them good advice.

B. Read the paragraph in Activity A again. Circle *but*.

Writing Strategy

Compound sentences with *but*
A compound sentence shows a relationship between two ideas. Write a compound sentence with *but* to show difference.

> *My sister spends her money on jewelry, **but** I always buy computer games.*
> (a difference between my sister and me)

> *Martha works hard, **but** she makes a lot of money.*
> (a difference between something difficult and something good)

Sometimes the verb after *but* is negative (*does not* + verb).

> *Jose <u>buys</u> cheap clothes, but he <u>does not buy</u> cheap electronics.*
> *She <u>likes</u> expensive jewelry, but she <u>does not pay</u> full price.*

GO ONLINE
for more
practice

C. Circle *and* or *but*. Write the correct sentences below.

1. He knows about good deals, (and) *but* he does not pay full price.

   He knows about good deals, and he does not pay full price.

2. I listen to music, *and but* I buy music online.

   _____

3. She learns about fashion online, *and but* she buys her clothes in stores.

   _____

4. I look at products in stores, *and but* I compare prices.

   _____

5. My friend goes to nice restaurants, *and but* he spends a lot of money on food.

   _____

D. Rewrite your paragraph from page 104. Use the questions below to help you.

Revising Questions

Can you:

- use *but* to show a difference?

- add vocabulary words?

- add ideas?

Oxford 2000 🔑

Do you need more words to write about someone who gets a good deal? Use the Oxford 2000 list on page 133 to find more words for your sentences.

Step 5 EDIT

Writing Strategy

Using *for example*

Use *for example* when you give details to explain an idea. *For example* often answers the question *How?*

How does he get good deals?

He gets good deals on computers. **For example**, he compares prices online.

How does she get information?

She finds out a lot about products. **For example**, she asks many questions.

Use *for example* at the beginning of a new sentence. Use a comma after *for example*.

She is organized. **For example,** she always makes plans.

GO ONLINE
for more practice

A. Match each topic sentence with the correct example sentence. Write the correct sentences below. Use *for example*.

Topic sentence		Example sentence
~~1. My friend knows a lot about clothes.~~		a. she visits many different countries and tries new food.
2. Neal is active.		b. she wears cheap shoes with expensive jewelry.
3. He gets good deals on electronics.	For example,	~~c. she reads about fashion.~~
4. My sister is busy.		d. he plays soccer and rides a bicycle.
5. She is an adventurous traveler.		e. she studies in the morning and works at night.
6. Gina likes clothes and combines different things.		f. he finds cheap computers online.

1. My friend knows a lot about clothes. For example, she reads about fashion.

2. _____

3. _____

4. _____

5. _____

6. _____

B. Explain each idea. Use *for example* with a sentence to explain *How?*

1. I get good deals on phones. For example, I never buy new phones.

2. He saves money on electronics. _____

3. She spends a lot of money on food. _____

4. I never buy expensive clothes. _____

5. They are social. _____

C. Read the following paragraph. Find and correct six mistakes. The first mistake is corrected for you.

My Mother's Shoes

My mother ~~know~~ knows a lot about shoes, for example she reads about fashion online, and she learns new shoes and clothes. She not like cheap shoes. She goes to famous stores in the city, and she buys expensive shoes. She fashionable, and she does not get good deals.

D. Read your paragraph again. Check (✓) the things in your paragraph.

Editing Checklist

○ 1. Capital letters
○ 2. Verbs + *about*
○ 3. Periods
○ 4. Compound sentences with *but*
○ 5. *does not* + verbs
○ 6. *for example*

E. Now write your final paragraph. Use the Editing Checklist to help you.

Step 6 PUBLISH

Follow these steps to publish your paragraph.

Publishing Steps

• Share your paragraph with a partner.

• Answer the questions.

  • What idea do you like in your partner's paragraph?

  • Are you similar to or different from the shopper in the paragraph?

• Put your paragraph in your portfolio!

CHAPTER 8

What Is Your Favorite Restaurant?

- Use *do not* + verbs
- Use *the* + nouns
- Use compound sentences with *so*

- Use *first*, *second*, and *third* to introduce different ideas
- Write a paragraph about your favorite restaurant

▲ VOCABULARY ▶ Oxford 2000 ✎ words to describe restaurants

A. Write the correct number from the pictures next to each item in the box.

_____ a popular place	_____ grilled meat	_____ servers	_____ spicy chicken
__1__ wait for a table	_____ share a meal	_____ eat a lot	_____ order lunch
_____ meet friends for dinner	_____ delicious vegetables		

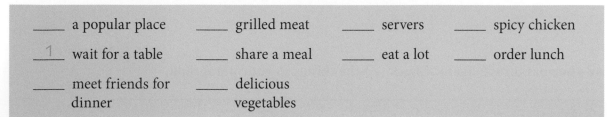

B. Write each phrase below the correct picture.

a crowded table	grilled vegetables	spicy food
order dinner	wait for a friend	friendly server

1.

grilled vegetables

2.

_____

3.

_____

4.

_____

5.

_____

6.

_____

Oxford 2000 🔑

Use the Oxford 2000 list on page 133 to find more words to describe the pictures on these pages. Share your words with a partner.

C. Circle the correct words.

1. fast   *restaurant*   *service*

2. polite   *food*   *servers*

3. delicious   *vegetables*   *table*

4. grilled   *experience*   *meat*

5. wait for   *dinner*   *fast service*

6. meet   *relatives*   *a meal*

GO ONLINE
for more
practice

A. Read the paragraph. Then look at the pictures. Check (✓) the picture that matches the paragraph.

River Café

River Café is my favorite restaurant. My sister and I often go there for dinner. We like it for three reasons. First, it is comfortable. The building is old, but it is beautiful. There are many customers, and we often see our neighbors there. We visit their table and talk. Second, River Café has good service. The servers are polite, and they know a lot about the food. Third, the food is delicious. I do not eat meat, so I order the seafood. My sister is different. She likes meat, so we do not share meals. We eat a lot, and we are happy.

Grammar Note

do not + verbs

Use *do not* + a verb after some nouns to show that something is not true.

Use *do not* + a verb after *I*.

   *I always order vegetables. I **do not eat** meat.*

Use *do not* + a verb after *We*.

   *We like the food. We **do not complain.***

Use *do not* + a verb after *They*.

   *The servers are careful. They **do not make** mistakes.*

GO ONLINE
for more
practice

B. Match the sentences. Write the letter of each explanation sentence in the blank.

1. __b__ The restaurant is not crowded.   a. I do not eat meat.

2. _____ My brothers like the service.   b. ~~People do not wait for a table.~~

3. _____ I order vegetables.   c. They do not eat dinner at home.

4. _____ My friends and I get a good deal.   d. They do not smile.

5. _____ The servers are not friendly.   e. We do not spend a lot of money.

6. _____ My parents always go to restaurants.   f. They do not complain about the servers.

C. Use the words in the chart to answer the questions. Write two more sentences for each question.

Customers		wait for a table
Servers		say hello to customers
People		get a good deal
I		forget the order
We	(do not)	work hard
They		recommend the restaurant
		eat a lot
		complain about the food
		try different food
		meet friends for dinner

1. What do you like about your favorite restaurant?

   a. _Servers say hello to customers._ _____

   b. _____

   c. _____

2. What happens in a bad restaurant?

   a. _Servers do not work hard._ _____

   b. _____

   c. _____

the + nouns

Use *the* before a noun to connect the noun to a specific place or thing.

The connects *food* with *Ping's*   *The* connects *service* with *Ping's*

We like Ping's. **The** food is delicious. **The** service is friendly.

Use *the* with specific noncount nouns.

The connects *seafood* with *Mrs. Mai's*

I like seafood. I order **the** seafood at Mrs. Mai's.

Use *the* with specific plural nouns.

the connects *vegetables* with *River Café*

I don't like vegetables, but at River Café, **the** vegetables are delicious.

Use *the* with specific singular nouns.

The connects *café* with *Cam's*

I meet my friends at Cam's. **The** café is friendly and cheap.

GO ONLINE
for more
practice

D. Complete each supporting sentence about Cam's Café. Then add a new sentence. Use *the* and your own ideas.

Topic Sentence: We recommend Cam's for many reasons.

1. The service <u>is good</u>_____.

<u>The servers work hard.</u>_____

2. The food _____.

_____

3. The prices _____.

_____

4. The building _____.

_____

E. Read the first sentence. Circle the letter of the correct supporting sentence.

1. I study at my school.
   a. The library is quiet.
   b. A library is quiet.

2. Empire Café serves good food.
   a. The grilled chicken is delicious.
   b. Grilled chicken is delicious.

3. I do not like restaurants.
   a. Food is boring.
   b. The food is boring.

4. Amy's has many customers, and it is often crowded.
   a. The customers do not complain. They like the service and the food.
   b. Customers do not complain. They like service and food.

5. The Grand Hotel has an expensive restaurant.
   a. The food is delicious, and the service is excellent.
   b. Food is delicious, and service is excellent.

F. Use the words in the chart to write sentences.

At Mrs. Mai's, we share the food.

At River Café, At Ahmed's, At Mrs. Mai's,	I we the customers they	(do not)	eat order like share	the food the seafood the spicy meat the grilled vegetables
	the servers		bring recommend	

1. _____

2. _____

3. _____

4. _____

Chant

GO ONLINE for the Chapter 8 Vocabulary & Grammar Chant

▲▲▲ WRITING
► Compound sentences with *so*
► Using *first*, *second*, and *third* to introduce different ideas

Writing Assignment Write a paragraph.

What is your favorite restaurant?

Step 1 PREPARE

A. Read Luan's paragraph. Do you know of a similar restaurant?

Mrs. Mai's

My friends and I like Mrs. Mai's for three reasons. First, the restaurant is comfortable. The music is quiet, so we can talk. Second, we like the food. For example, the spicy chicken is delicious, and the grilled vegetables are fresh. The servers bring a lot of food, so my friends and I often share meals. Third, the prices are good, so we do not spend a lot of money. We always feel happy at Mrs. Mai's.

B. Answer the questions below. Use information from Luan's paragraph.

1. What restaurant do Luan and his friends like?

_____

2. How many reasons does he give for liking the restaurant?

_____

3. What is the first reason Luan and his friends like Mrs. Mai's?

_____

4. What is the second reason they like it?

a. _____

b. What is an example? _____

5. What is the third reason they like it?

_____

6. How do they feel there?

_____

Step 2 PREWRITE

A. Write notes in the chart about a restaurant you recommend. Then circle two or three things that you want to write about.

The restaurant	The food	The servers	The prices

B. Write topic sentences about your restaurant. Choose one for your paragraph.

1. I recommend _____ for three reasons.

2. My favorite restaurant is _____.

3. My friends and I like _____ for many reasons.

Step 3 WRITE

A. Answer the questions. Write sentences using words from the chart above. Explain your reasons or give examples.

1. What is your favorite restaurant? (Write your topic sentence here.)

_____

2. What is your first reason?

_____

3. What is your second reason?

_____

4. What is the third reason?

_____

5. How do you feel at the restaurant?

_____

Word Partners

eat food

order food

bring food

recommend food

share food

like food

pay for good food

try new food

GO ONLINE
to practice
word partners

B. Use your sentences to write a paragraph in your notebook.

C. Add a title to your paragraph. _____

Step 4 REVISE

A. Read the paragraph. Is the restaurant for your paragraph similar or different?

Kebab House

My friends and I like Kebab House. We often meet for lunch. It is a good place for many reasons. First, it is fast. The restaurant is near our school. We walk there and get food fast. Second, it is not expensive. We are students, so we are careful with money. Third, Kebab House has good food. The restaurant serves different kinds of grilled meat, and it is always delicious. We eat a lot, and we feel happy.

B. Read the paragraph in Activity A again. Circle _so_.

Writing Strategy

Compound sentences with _so_

A compound sentence shows a relationship between two ideas. Write a compound sentence with _so_ to show cause and then effect.

cause		effect

My mother does not like chicken, **so** _we eat a lot of seafood._

cause		effect

I do not like the food, **so** _I do not go to Harry's Café._

Use a comma and then _so_. Do not capitalize _so_.

The café is not expensive, **so** _we get a good deal._

GO ONLINE
for more
practice

C. Circle the letter to complete each sentence with *so*.

1. The restaurant is expensive, so

   a. we often go there.

   b. we spend a lot of money.

2. There are always many customers, so

   a. they have rice and vegetables.

   b. the servers are busy.

3. I do not like seafood, so

   a. I order seafood and rice.

   b. I order meat and vegetables.

4. Pierre's is expensive, so

   a. customers do not eat at home.

   b. customers spend a lot of money.

D. Complete the sentences with effects.

1. There are many customers, so the waiters are busy   .

2. I do not like chicken, so _____.

3. The café is quiet, so _____.

4. The servers are polite, so _____.

5. The restaurant has delicious food, so _____.

6. The restaurant is big, so _____.

E. Rewrite your paragraph from page 116. Use the questions below to help you.

Revising Questions

Can you:

- use *so* to show an effect?

- add vocabulary words?

- add ideas?

Oxford 2000 🔑

Do you need more words to write about your favorite restaurant? Use the Oxford 2000 list on page 133 to find more words for your sentences.

Writing Strategy

Using *first*, *second*, and *third* to introduce different ideas

Use *first*, *second*, and *third* to introduce new supporting ideas.

1 = First	**First**, *the restaurant is beautiful.*
2 = Second	**Second**, *the restaurant has good food.*
3 = Third	**Third**, *the restaurant has polite servers.*

Use a comma after *first*, *second*, and *third* at the beginning of a sentence.

GO ONLINE
for more
practice

A. Write the following sentences as a short paragraph. Change the numbers to *first*, *second*, and *third*.

Topic sentence: I like the restaurant in the Grand Hotel for three reasons.

Supporting sentences: 1. The hotel is beautiful. The building is historic.

2. The customers are fashionable. They wear expensive clothes.

3. It has good food. The dinners are delicious.

_____

_____

_____

B. Add *first*, *second*, and *third* to the following paragraphs.

1.

First, t

I recommend Red's. The servers give customers a lot of food, and it is delicious. The meat is spicy, and the seafood is fresh. The servers are friendly. They smile and talk to customers. The prices are good. Customers do not complain. They are always happy.

2.

My family and I like the Starlight Café for three reasons. I know the servers. They are friendly, so my children feel comfortable. The meals are delicious. I recommend the grilled chicken with vegetables. The Starlight Café is a quiet place. We do not like crowded restaurants. The Starlight Café is peaceful, so we talk and have a nice dinner.

C. Read the paragraph below. Find and correct six mistakes. The first mistake is corrected for you.

Paco's

the

I recommend Paco's for three reasons. First, restaurant is beautiful. It

is modern so the servers wear nice clothes. Second the food is delicious.

The grilled seafood is popular, and spicy chicken is delicious. third,

important people eat at Paco's. Customers wear fashionable clothes and

expensive jewelry. I like Paco's, so do not complain about the prices.

D. Read your paragraph again. Check (✓) the things in your paragraph.

Editing Checklist

○ 1. Capital letters   ○ 2. *the* + noun

○ 3. Periods   ○ 4. Compound sentences with *so*

○ 5. *do not* + verbs   ○ 6. *first, second,* and *third*

E. Now write your final paragraph. Use the Editing Checklist to help you.

Step 6 PUBLISH

Follow these steps to publish your paragraph.

Publishing Steps

• Share your paragraph with two partners.

• Answer the questions.

   • What restaurant do you like?

   • How is your restaurant similar to or different from each of your partner's restaurants?

• Put your paragraph in your portfolio!

CHAPTER 9 — Where Do You Want to Go?

- Use *want to* + verbs
- Use the present progressive
- Use *right now* to change focus
- Learn about spelling verbs with *-ing*
- Write a paragraph about a place you want to visit

▲ VOCABULARY ▶ Oxford 2000 🔑 words to describe travel plans

A. Write the correct number from the pictures next to each item in the box.

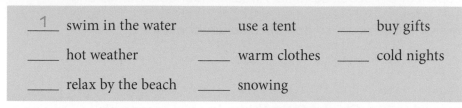

_1_ swim in the water ⎯⎯ use a tent ⎯⎯ buy gifts

⎯⎯ hot weather ⎯⎯ warm clothes ⎯⎯ cold nights

⎯⎯ relax by the beach ⎯⎯ snowing

1. ⎯⎯⎯⎯⎯⎯⎯⎯⎯⎯⎯⎯⎯⎯⎯⎯ 2. ⎯⎯⎯⎯⎯⎯⎯⎯⎯⎯⎯⎯⎯⎯⎯⎯

B. Match each sentence below to one of the pictures above. Write the sentence below the picture.

I'm planning a trip next winter. I'm planning a trip next summer.

C. Write each word below the correct picture to complete the phrase.

gift	tea	weather	water	nature	adventure

1.

give a _____ gift _____

2.

swim in the _____

Oxford 2000 🔑

Use the Oxford 2000 list on page 133 to find more words to describe the pictures on these pages. Share your words with a partner.

3.

drink hot _____

4.

relax in _____

5.

cold _____

6.

an interesting _____

D. Write *summer* or *winter* next to each sentence.

1. Families bring food to the park at night. _____ summer _____

2. Many people complain about cold weather. _____ winter _____

3. People do not wear warm clothes. _____

4. People like hot drinks. _____

5. The weather is nice, so people walk on the streets at night. _____

6. People swim in the ocean. _____

7. Children play in the water. _____

GO ONLINE for more practice

A. Read Jose's paragraph. Where is he planning to go?

A Trip to the Beach

I am planning a trip to the ocean next summer. My family and I live in a cold place. It snows a lot, so we want to visit a warm country. We want to stay in a hotel by the beach. My parents want to try new food, and I want to swim in the ocean. My sisters want to buy interesting gifts for their friends. Right now, we are making travel plans. We are reading about different places, and we are learning about the weather, food, and prices.

B. Read the sentences about the paragraph in Activity A. Write *T* (true), *F* (false), or *?* (don't know).

__F__ 1. Jose wants to go to the ocean next winter.

_____ 2. Jose does not like cold weather.

_____ 3. His parents want to swim.

_____ 4. They are learning about the weather at the beach.

_____ 5. His sisters are saving money for gifts.

Grammar Note

want to + verbs

Use *want to* with a verb to explain a strong feeling about a plan or goal you have.

Use *want to* with a verb after *I, we,* and *they*.

> *I* **want to go** to the beach
> *We* **want to visit** Hong Kong.
> *They* **want to buy** gifts for their friends.

Use *wants to* with a verb after *he* and *she*.

> *He* **wants to relax** by the beach.
> *She* **wants to buy** gifts.

Use *do/does not want to* with a verb to show negative.

> *I* **do not want to swim** in the ocean.
> *He* **does not want to spend** a lot of money.

GO ONLINE
for more
practice

C. Read the sentences below. Write a supporting sentence with *want to* or *wants to* and the words in the box.

buy new shoes	save money	visit a warm country	try different restaurants
go home	see mountains		

1. My brother likes food. He wants to try different restaurants.

2. My sister is saving money. _____

3. He is reading about cheap hotels. _____

4. I like adventures in nature. _____

5. My friend misses his country. _____

6. I don't like cold weather. _____

D. Read the sentences. Complete each sentence with *do not want to* or *does not want to* and the words in the box to show an effect.

wear warm clothes	forget her map	eat a big dinner
buy expensive gifts	swim in the ocean	wait for a table

1. They are busy, so they do not want to wait for a table.

2. I do not have a lot of money, so I _____

3. I always eat a big lunch, so I _____

4. She does not want to get lost, so she _____

5. He does not like water, so he _____

6. We are visiting a hot country, so we _____

E. Think about your next trip. Circle your answer to the question. Ask your classmate. Then write sentences about you and your classmate. Are you different or similar?

1. Where do you want to visit?   *the ocean   the mountains   a big city*

   Me: I want to visit a big city.

   My classmate: My classmate wants to visit the mountains.

2. What do you want to see?   *beaches   green forests   interesting streets*

   Me: _____

   My classmate: _____

3. What do you want to do?   *see nature   swim   shop in famous stores*

Me: _____

My classmate: _____

4. What do you want to eat?   *seafood   meat   vegetables*

Me: _____

My classmate: _____

5. What do you want to buy?   *clothes   electronics   jewelry*

Me: _____

My classmate: _____

6. Who do you want to travel with?   *my friends   one friend   my family*

Me: _____

My classmate: _____

Grammar Note

Present progressive

The present progressive uses *am/is/are* with a verb + *ing* to focus on actions that are true for a period of time right now but are not always true.

I have many books.   *Right now, I **am reading** a book about South Africa.*
(true for a long time, a fact) (There is a change. Something is true right now.)

Use *am* with a verb + *-ing* after *I*.

> *I **am planning** a trip.*
> *I **am learning** about South Africa right now.*

Use *is* with a verb + *-ing* after *he*, *she*, and *it*.

> *He **is ordering** dinner.*
> *She **is eating** hot soup.*
> *It **is snowing**.*

Use *are* with a verb + *-ing* after *we* and *they*.

> *We **are reading** about hotels.*
> *They **are sharing** a meal.*

Use *am/is/are* + *not* with a verb + *-ing* for a negative statement.

> *I **am not eating** in restaurants.*
> *She **is not shopping** in expensive stores.*
> *My children **are not complaining**.*

GO ONLINE
for more
practice

F. Nabil wants to save money for a trip, so his life is different right now. Use *he is* and *he is not* with verb + *-ing* to write sentences.

1. buying cheap food

He is buying cheap food.

2. eating in expensive restaurants

_____

3. comparing prices

_____

4. shopping at expensive stores

_____

5. saving money

_____

G. Complete the sentences. Use words and phrases from the box.

I	am	buying warm clothes
		learning about the weather and money
He	is	making travel plans
She		planning a trip to London
It		saving money
		talking to family about the trip
We	are	using a map
They		wearing comfortable shoes

1. My friends and I want to visit Japan, so we are learning about the weather and money .

2. He wants to go to a cold place, so _____.

3. My parents want to see a big city, so _____.

4. They are walking, so _____.

5. I want to take an expensive trip, so _____.

6. My sister is an organized traveler, so _____.

Chant

GO ONLINE
for the
Chapter 9
Vocabulary &
Grammar Chant

▲▲▲ WRITING
▶ Using *right now* to change focus
▶ Spelling verbs with *-ing*

Writing Assignment Write a paragraph.

Where do you want to go?

Step 1 PREPARE

A. Read Natalya's paragraph. Is this trip interesting to you? Why or why not?

> ## Winter in the Mountains
>
> My friends and I are planning a trip to the mountains next winter. We do not want to have a boring trip. We want to have an adventure. We want to stay in the forest, walk to lakes, and see beautiful nature. Right now, we are planning our trip. The weather is cold in the mountains. It snows a lot, so we are shopping for warm clothes and shoes. We are reading books about nature and planning our meals.

B. Answer the questions about Natalya's paragraph.

1. What trip is the writer planning?

_____

2. Who is she going with? When?

_____

3. What does she want to do?

    a. _____

    b. _____

    c. _____

4. Right now, what plans is she making?

    a. _____

    b. _____

Step 2 PREWRITE

A. Check (✓) a trip you want to take. Circle *next summer* or *next winter*.

☐ to the beach   *next summer*   *next winter*

☐ to the mountains   *next summer*   *next winter*

☐ to a big city   *next summer*   *next winter*

☐ to a new country   *next summer*   *next winter*

B. Complete the topic sentences. Then check (✓) the topic sentence you want to use for your paragraph.

1. I am planning a trip to _____.

2. I want to go to _____.

C. What do you want to do, and what plans are you making right now? Write ideas in the chart.

I want to/We want to...	I am/We are...

Step 3 WRITE

A. Answer the questions. Write sentences using words from the chart above.

1. Where do you want to go?

_____

2. Who are you going with? When?

_____

3. What do you (and others) want to do?

_____

4. Right now, what plans are you making?

_____

✎ **B. Use your sentences to write a paragraph in your notebook.**

✎ **C. Add a title to your paragraph.** _____

Word Partners

warm weather

warm clothes

warm shoes

warm water

warm night

GO ONLINE
to practice
word partners

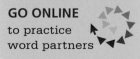

A. Read the paragraph. What do you like about this trip?

A Trip Home

I am planning a trip to my country next summer. I want to see my family and my childhood home. I miss my street. There are tall, green trees, and children play soccer. I want to sit outside with my family and see my old neighbors. We want to share stories about our adventures. I want to walk by the river and meet my friends at a café at night. Right now, I am planning. I am shopping for gifts. I want to buy jewelry for my mother and sister, and I want to buy electronics for my father and brothers.

B. Read the paragraph in Activity A again. Circle *right now*.

GO ONLINE
for more
practice

Writing Strategy

Using *right now* to change focus
Use *right now* with the present progressive to show a change in focus.

      always true   New focus: The action is true now but not always true.
I like nature. **Right now**, *I am reading a book about mountains.*

      always true   New focus: The action is true now but not always true.
I want to visit Singapore. **Right now**, *I am saving money.*

Right now is often used at the beginning of a sentence. Use a comma after *right now*.

C. Write the sentences as a paragraph. Add *right now* to show a change of focus.

1. My parents want to visit me.

   They want to see my school.

   They are asking me questions.

   They want to bring me gifts.

   My parents want to visit me. They want to see my school. Right now, they are asking me questions. They want to bring me gifts.

2. My friends and I love soccer.

   We want to go to Spain and watch soccer games.

   We are saving money for our trip.

   For example, we are not spending money on restaurants.

   _____

   _____

   _____

3. My sisters and I like nature.

   We want to stay by a beautiful lake.

   We are reading about different hotels.

   We are comparing prices.

   _____

   _____

   _____

4. My brother wants to visit the desert next summer.

   He is reading a lot of books.

   He is learning new things about the desert.

   For example, it is hot, but it is cold at night.

   _____

   _____

   _____

D. Complete the sentences below. Use the present progressive and the words in the box.

| spend/money on a new bicycle | talk/to my friends about travel plans |
| ~~go/to a café~~ | wait/for a table at a famous restaurant |

1. My sister and I want to have coffee and talk. Right now, _we are going to a café_.

2. She wants to eat good food. Right now, _____.

3. I want to have an interesting adventure. Right now, _____.

4. My brother wants to ride a bicycle in nature. Right now, _____.

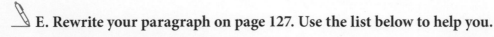 **E. Rewrite your paragraph on page 127. Use the list below to help you.**

Oxford 2000 🔑

Do you need more words to write about travel plans? Use the Oxford 2000 list on page 133 to find more words for your sentences.

Revising Questions

Can you:

- use *right now* to show a change of focus?
- add vocabulary words?
- add ideas?

Step 5 EDIT

Writing Strategy

Spelling verbs with *-ing*

Many verbs end in *e*. When you add *-ing*, do not use *e*.

I am taking a trip.   NOT: ~~I am takeing a trip.~~

Here are some other examples.

give → giving   smile → smiling
ride → riding   take → taking
save → saving   use → using
compare → comparing

Some verbs change in a different way. They take two letters + *-ing*. The following are some examples:

shop → shopping   get → getting
plan → planning   swim → swimming

GO ONLINE
for more
practice

A. Combine the verb with *-ing*. Write the verb. Use correct spelling.

1. relax + *-ing*: _____relaxing_____

2. give + *-ing*: _____giving_____

3. use + *-ing*: _____

4. ride + *-ing*: _____

5. swim + *-ing*: _____

6. shop + *-ing*: _____

B. Read the paragraph below. Find and correct six mistakes. The first mistake is corrected for you.

An Expensive Trip

I want to visit Thailand. I want ^to^ visit beautiful cities. I want see beautiful beaches. I want to eat in expensive restaurants. Right now, I am saveing money. I am use the Internet, and I am geting deals on hotels. I sharing a room with friends.

C. Read your paragraph again. Check (✓) the things in your paragraph.

Editing Checklist

○ 1. Capital letters and periods   ○ 2. *right now* to show a change of focus

○ 3. *want to* + verb   ○ 4. Correct spelling of verbs with *-ing*

○ 5. Present progressive

D. Now write your final paragraph. Use the Editing Checklist to help you.

Step 6 PUBLISH

Follow these steps to publish your paragraph.

Publishing Steps

- Share your paragraph with a partner.
- Answer the questions.
  - What sentences do you like in your partner's paragraph?
  - Do you like your partner's plan for a trip? Explain.
- Put your paragraph in your portfolio!

Look at the word bank for Unit 3. Check (✓) the words you know. Circle the words you want to learn better.

OXFORD 2000 🔑				
Adjectives	**Nouns**		**Verbs**	
cheap	adventure	shoe	compare	relax
cold	advice	summer	give	save
expensive	deal	table	go home	snow
fast	dinner	tea	know (about)	swim
full	gift	technology	learn	wait
hot	jewelry	vegetable	order	
next	lunch	water		
popular	meal	weather		
warm	meat	winter		
	product			

PRACTICE WITH THE OXFORD 2000 🔑

A. Use the chart. Match adjectives with nouns.

1. _____cheap jewelry_____   2. _____

3. _____   4. _____

5. _____   6. _____

B. Use the chart. Match verbs with nouns.

1. _____compare deals_____   2. _____

3. _____   4. _____

5. _____   6. _____

C. Use the chart. Match verbs with adjective noun partners.

1. _know about expensive shoes_   2. _____

3. _____   4. _____

5. _____   6. _____

GO ONLINE
for more
practice

THE OXFORD 2000 ♪ LIST OF KEYWORDS

This is a list of the 2000 most important and useful words to learn at this stage in your language learning. These words have been carefully chosen by a group of language experts and experienced teachers, who have judged the words to be important and useful for three reasons.

- Words that are used very **frequently** (= very often) in English are included in this list. Frequency information has been gathered from the American English section of the Oxford English Corpus, which is a collection of written and spoken texts containing over 2 billion words.

- The keywords are frequent across a **range** of different types of text. This means that the keywords are often used in a variety of contexts, not just in newspapers or in scientific articles for example.

- The list includes some important words which are very **familiar** to most users of English, even though they are not used very frequently. These include, for example, words which are useful for explaining what you mean when you do not know the exact word for something.

Names of people, places, etc. beginning with a capital letter are not included in the list of 2000 keywords. Keywords which are not included in the list are numbers, days of the week, and the months of the year.

A

a, an *indefinite article*
ability *n.*
able *adj.*
about *adv., prep.*
above *prep., adv.*
absolutely *adv.*
academic *adj.*
accept *v.*
acceptable *adj.*
accident *n.*
  by accident
according to prep.
account *n.*
accurate *adj.*
accuse *v.*
achieve *v.*
achievement *n.*
acid *n.*
across *adv., prep.*
act *n., v.*
action *n.*
active *adj.*
activity *n.*
actor, actress *n.*
actual *adj.*
actually *adv.*
add *v.*
address *n.*
admire *v.*
admit *v.*
adult *n.*
advanced *adj.*
advantage *n.*
adventure *n.*
advertisement *n.*
advice *n.*

advise *v.*
affect *v.*
afford *v.*
afraid *adj.*
after *prep., conj., adv.*
afternoon *n.*
afterward *adv.*
again *adv.*
against *prep.*
age *n.*
  aged *adj.*
ago *adv.*
agree *v.*
agreement *n.*
ahead *adv.*
aim *n., v.*
air *n.*
airplane *n.*
airport *n.*
alarm *n.*
alcohol *n.*
alcoholic *adj.*
alive *adj.*
all *adj., pron., adv.*
allow *v.*
all right *adj., adv.,*
  exclamation
almost *adv.*
alone *adj., adv.*
along *prep., adv.*
alphabet *n.*
already *adv.*
also *adv.*
although *conj.*
always *adv.*
among *prep.*
amount *n.*

amuse *v.*
analyze *v.*
analysis *n.*
ancient *adj.*
and *conj.*
anger *n.*
angle *n.*
angry *adj.*
animal *n.*
announce *v.*
another *adj., pron.*
answer *n., v.*
any *adj., pron., adv.*
anymore *(also* any more*)*
  adv.
anyone *(also* anybody*)*
  pron.
anything *pron.*
anyway *adv.*
anywhere *adv.*
apart *adv.*
apartment *n.*
apparently *adv.*
appear *v.*
appearance *n.*
apple *n.*
apply *v.*
appointment *n.*
appreciate *v.*
appropriate *adj.*
approve *v.*
area *n.*
argue *v.*
argument *n.*
arm *n.*
army *n.*
around *adv., prep.*

arrange *v.*
arrangement *n.*
arrest *v.*
arrive *v.*
arrow *n.*
art *n.*
article *n.*
artificial *adj.*
artist *n.*
artistic *adj.*
as *prep., conj.*
ashamed *adj.*
ask *v.*
asleep *adj.*
at *prep.*
atmosphere *n.*
atom *n.*
attach *v.*
attack *n., v.*
attention *n.*
attitude *n.*
attract *v.*
attractive *adj.*
aunt *n.*
authority *n.*
available *adj.*
average *adj., n.*
avoid *v.*
awake *adj.*
aware *adj.*
away *adv.*

B

baby *n.*
back *n., adj., adv.*
backward *adv.*
bad *adj.*

badly *adv.*
bag *n.*
bake *v.*
balance *n.*
ball *n.*
band *n.*
bank *n.*
bar *n.*
base *n., v.*
baseball *n.*
basic *adj.*
basis *n.*
bath *n.*
bathroom *n.*
be *v.*
beach *n.*
bear *v.*
beard *n.*
beat *v.*
beautiful *adj.*
beauty *n.*
because *conj.*
become *v.*
bed *n.*
bedroom *n.*
beer *n.*
before *prep., conj., adv.*
begin *v.*
beginning *n.*
behave *v.*
behavior *n.*
behind *prep., adv.*
belief *n.*
believe *v.*
bell *n.*
belong *v.*
below *prep., adv.*
belt *n.*
bend *v.*
benefit *n.*
beside *prep.*
best *adj., adv., n.*
better *adj., adv.*
between *prep., adv.*
beyond *prep., adv.*
bicycle *n.*
big *adj.*
bill *n.*
bird *n.*
birth *n.*
birthday *n.*
bite *v.*
bitter *adj.*
black *adj.*
blame *v.*
block *n.*
blood *n.*
blow *v., n.*
blue *adj., n.*

board *n.*
boat *n.*
body *n.*
boil *v.*
bomb *n., v.*
bone *n.*
book *n.*
boot *n.*
border *n.*
bored *adj.*
boring *adj.*
born: be born *v.*
borrow *v.*
boss *n.*
both *adj., pron.*
bother *v.*
bottle *n.*
bottom *n.*
bowl *n.*
box *n.*
boy *n.*
boyfriend *n.*
brain *n.*
branch *n.*
brave *adj.*
bread *n.*
break *v.*
breakfast *n.*
breath *n.*
breathe *v.*
brick *n.*
bridge *n.*
brief *adj.*
bright *adj.*
bring *v.*
broken *adj.*
brother *n.*
brown *adj., n.*
brush *n., v.*
bubble *n.*
build *v.*
building *n.*
bullet *n.*
burn *v.*
burst *v.*
bury *v.*
bus *n.*
bush *n.*
business *n.*
busy *adj.*
but *conj.*
butter *n.*
button *n.*
buy *v.*
by *prep.*
bye *exclamation*

C

cabinet *n.*

cake *n.*
calculate *v.*
call *v., n.*
calm *adj.*
camera *n.*
camp *n., v.*
can *modal v., n.*
cancel *v.*
candy *n.*
capable *adj.*
capital *n.*
car *n.*
card *n.*
care *n., v.*
   take care of
   care for
career *n.*
careful *adj.*
carefully *adv.*
careless *adj.*
carelessly *adv.*
carry *v.*
case *n.*
   in case (of)
cash *n.*
cat *n.*
catch *v.*
cause *n., v.*
CD *n.*
ceiling *n.*
celebrate *v.*
cell *n.*
cell phone *n.*
cent *n.*
center *n.*
centimeter *n.*
central *adj.*
century *n.*
ceremony *n.*
certain *adj.*
certainly *adv.*
chain *n., v.*
chair *n.*
challenge *n.*
chance *n.*
change *v., n.*
character *n.*
characteristic *n.*
charge *n., v.*
charity *n.*
chase *v., n.*
cheap *adj.*
cheat *v.*
check *v., n.*
cheek *n.*
cheese *n.*
chemical *adj., n.*
chemistry *n.*
chest *n.*

chicken *n.*
chief *adj., n.*
child *n.*
childhood *n.*
chin *n.*
chocolate *n.*
choice *n.*
choose *v.*
church *n.*
cigarette *n.*
circle *n.*
citizen *n.*
city *n.*
class *n.*
clean *adj., v.*
clear *adj., v.*
clearly *adv.*
climate *n.*
climb *v.*
clock *n.*
close /kloʊs/ *adj., adv.*
close /kloʊz/ *v.*
closed *adj.*
cloth *n.*
clothes *n.*
clothing *n.*
cloud *n.*
club *n.*
coast *n.*
coat *n.*
coffee *n.*
coin *n.*
cold *adj., n.*
collect *v.*
collection *n.*
college *n.*
color *n., v.*
column *n.*
combination *n.*
combine *v.*
come *v.*
comfortable *adj.*
command *n.*
comment *n., v.*
common *adj.*
communicate *v.*
communication *n.*
community *n.*
company *n.*
compare *v.*
comparison *n.*
competition *n.*
complain *v.*
complaint *n.*
complete *adj.*
completely *adv.*
complicated *adj.*
computer *n.*
concentrate *v.*

concert *n.*
conclusion *n.*
condition *n.*
confidence *n.*
confident *adj.*
confuse *v.*
confused *adj.*
connect *v.*
connection *n.*
conscious *adj.*
consider *v.*
consist *v.*
constant *adj.*
contact *n., v.*
contain *v.*
container *n.*
continent *n.*
continue *v.*
continuous *adj.*
contract *n.*
contrast *n.*
contribute *v.*
control *n., v.*
convenient *adj.*
conversation *n.*
convince *v.*
cook *v.*
cookie *n.*
cooking *n.*
cool *adj.*
copy *n., v.*
corner *n.*
correct *adj., v.*
correctly *adv.*
cost *n., v.*
cotton *n.*
cough *v.*
could *modal v.*
count *v.*
country *n.*
county *n.*
couple *n.*
course *n.*
    of course
court *n.*
cousin *n.*
cover *v., n.*
covering *n.*
cow *n.*
crack *v.*
crash *n., v.*
crazy *adj.*
cream *n., adj.*
create *v.*
credit card *n.*
crime *n.*
criminal *adj., n.*
crisis *n.*
criticism *n.*

criticize *v.*
cross *v.*
crowd *n.*
cruel *adj.*
crush *v.*
cry *v.*
culture *n.*
cup *n.*
curly *adj.*
curve *n.*
curved *adj.*
custom *n.*
customer *n.*
cut *v., n.*

D
dad *n.*
damage *n., v.*
dance *n., v.*
dancer *n.*
danger *n.*
dangerous *adj.*
dark *adj., n.*
date *n.*
daughter *n.*
day *n.*
dead *adj.*
deal *v.*
dear *adj.*
death *n.*
debt *n.*
decide *v.*
decision *n.*
decorate *v.*
deep *adj.*
deeply *adv.*
defeat *v.*
definite *adj.*
definitely *adv.*
definition *n.*
degree *n.*
deliberately *adv.*
deliver *v.*
demand *n., v.*
dentist *n.*
deny *v.*
department *n.*
depend *v.*
depression *n.*
describe *v.*
description *n.*
desert *n.*
deserve *v.*
design *n., v.*
desk *n.*
despite *prep.*
destroy *v.*
detail *n.*
    in detail

determination *n.*
determined *adj.*
develop *v.*
development *n.*
device *n.*
diagram *n.*
dictionary *n.*
die *v.*
difference *n.*
different *adj.*
difficult *adj.*
difficulty *n.*
dig *v.*
dinner *n.*
direct *adj., adv., v.*
direction *n.*
directly *adv.*
dirt *n.*
dirty *adj.*
disadvantage *n.*
disagree *v.*
disagreement *n.*
disappear *v.*
disappoint *v.*
disaster *n.*
discover *v.*
discuss *v.*
discussion *n.*
disease *n.*
disgusting *adj.*
dish *n.*
dishonest *adj.*
disk *n.*
distance *n.*
distant *adj.*
disturb *v.*
divide *v.*
division *n.*
divorce *n., v.*
do *v., auxiliary v.*
doctor *n. (abbr.* Dr.)
document *n.*
dog *n.*
dollar *n.*
door *n.*
dot *n.*
double *adj.*
doubt *n.*
down *adv., prep.*
downstairs *adv., adj.*
downward *adv.*
draw *v.*
drawer *n.*
drawing *n*
dream *n., v.*
dress *n., v.*
drink *n., v.*
drive *v., n.*
driver *n.*

drop *v., n.*
drug *n.*
dry *adj., v.*
during *prep.*
dust *n.*
duty *n.*
DVD *n.*

E
each *adj., pron.*
each other *pron.*
ear *n.*
early *adj., adv.*
earn *v.*
earth *n.*
easily *adv.*
east *n., adj., adv.*
eastern *adj.*
easy *adj.*
eat *v.*
economic *adj.*
economy *n.*
edge *n.*
educate *v.*
education *n.*
effect *n.*
effort *n.*
e.g. *abbr.*
egg *n.*
either *adj., pron., adv.*
election *n.*
electric *adj.*
electrical *adj.*
electricity *n.*
electronic *adj.*
else *adv.*
e-mail *(also* email*) n., v.*
embarrass *v.*
embarrassed *adj.*
emergency *n.*
emotion *n.*
employ *v.*
employment *n.*
empty *adj.*
encourage *v.*
end *n., v.*
    in the end
enemy *n.*
energy *n.*
engine *n.*
enjoy *v.*
enjoyable *adj.*
enjoyment *n.*
enough *adj., pron., adv.*
enter *v.*
entertain *v.*
entertainment *n.*
enthusiasm *n.*
enthusiastic *adj.*

The Oxford 2000 List of Keywords

entrance *n.*
environment *n.*
equal *adj.*
equipment *n.*
error *n.*
escape *v.*
especially *adv.*
essential *adj.*
etc. *abbr.*
even *adv.*
evening *n.*
event *n.*
ever *adv.*
every *adj.*
everybody *pron.*
everyone *pron.*
everything *pron.*
everywhere *adv.*
evidence *n.*
evil *adj.*
exact *adj.*
exactly *adv.*
exaggerate *v.*
exam *n.*
examination *n.*
examine *v.*
example *n.*
excellent *adj.*
except *prep.*
exchange *v., n.*
excited *adj.*
excitement *n.*
exciting *adj.*
excuse *n., v.*
exercise *n.*
exist *v.*
exit *n.*
expect *v.*
expensive *adj.*
experience *n., v.*
experiment *n.*
expert *n.*
explain *v.*
explanation *n.*
explode *v.*
explore *v.*
explosion *n.*
expression *n.*
extra *adj., adv.*
extreme *adj.*
extremely *adv.*
eye *n.*

F

face *n., v.*
fact *n.*
factory *n.*
fail *v.*
failure *n.*

fair *adj.*
fall *v., n.*
false *adj.*
familiar *adj.*
family *n.*
famous *adj.*
far *adv., adj.*
farm *n.*
farmer *n.*
fashion *n.*
fashionable *adj.*
fast *adj., adv.*
fasten *v.*
fat *adj., n.*
father *n.*
fault *n.*
favor *n.*
  in favor
favorite *adj., n.*
fear *n., v.*
feather *n.*
feature *n.*
feed *v.*
feel *v.*
feeling *n.*
female *adj.*
fence *n.*
festival *n.*
few *adj., pron.*
  a few
field *n.*
fight *v., n.*
figure *n.*
file *n.*
fill *v.*
film *n.*
final *adj.*
finally *adv.*
financial *adj.*
find *v.*
  find out sth
fine *adj.*
finger *n.*
finish *v.*
fire *n., v.*
firm *n., adj.*
firmly *adv.*
first *adj., adv., n.*
  at first
fish *n.*
fit *v., adj.*
fix *v.*
fixed *adj.*
flag *n.*
flame *n.*
flash *v.*
flat *adj.*
flavor *n.*
flight *n.*

float *v.*
flood *n.*
floor *n.*
flour *n.*
flow *v.*
flower *n.*
fly *v.*
fold *v.*
follow *v.*
food *n.*
foot *n.*
football *n.*
for *prep.*
force *n., v.*
foreign *adj.*
forest *n.*
forever *adv.*
forget *v.*
forgive *v.*
fork *n.*
form *n., v.*
formal *adj.*
forward *adv.*
frame *n.*
free *adj., v., adv.*
freedom *n.*
freeze *v.*
fresh *adj.*
friend *n.*
friendly *adj.*
friendship *n.*
frighten *v.*
from *prep.*
front *n., adj.*
  in front
frozen *adj.*
fruit *n.*
fry *v.*
fuel *n.*
full *adj.*
fully *adv.*
fun *n., adj.*
funny *adj.*
fur *n.*
furniture *n.*
further *adj., adv.*
future *n., adj.*

G

gain *v.*
gallon *n.*
game *n.*
garbage *n.*
garden *n.*
gas *n.*
gate *n.*
general *adj.*
  in general
generally *adv.*

generous *adj.*
gentle *adj.*
gently *adv.*
gentleman *n.*
get *v.*
gift *n.*
girl *n.*
girlfriend *n.*
give *v.*
glass *n.*
glasses *n.*
global *adj.*
glove *n.*
go *v.*
goal *n.*
god *n.*
gold *n., adj.*
good *adj., n.*
goodbye *exclamation*
goods *n.*
govern *v.*
government *n.*
grade *n., v.*
grain *n.*
gram *n.*
grammar *n.*
grandchild *n.*
grandfather *n.*
grandmother *n.*
grandparent *n.*
grass *n.*
grateful *adj.*
gray *adj., n.*
great *adj.*
green *adj., n.*
groceries *n.*
ground *n.*
group *n.*
grow *v.*
growth *n.*
guard *n., v.*
guess *v.*
guest *n.*
guide *n.*
guilty *adj.*
gun *n.*

H

habit *n.*
hair *n.*
half *n., adj., pron., adv.*
hall *n.*
hammer *n.*
hand *n.*
handle *v., n.*
hang *v.*
happen *v.*
happiness *n.*
happy *adj.*

hard *adj., adv.*
hardly *adv.*
harm *n., v.*
harmful *adj.*
hat *n.*
hate *v., n.*
have *v.*
    have to *modal v.*
he *pron.*
head *n.*
health *n.*
healthy *adj.*
hear *v.*
heart *n.*
heat *n., v.*
heavy *adj.*
height *n.*
hello *exclamation*
help *v., n.*
helpful *adj.*
her *pron., adj.*
here *adv.*
hers *pron.*
herself *pron.*
hide *v.*
high *adj., adv.*
highly *adv.*
high school *n.*
highway *n.*
hill *n.*
him *pron.*
himself *pron.*
hire *v.*
his *adj., pron.*
history *n.*
hit *v., n.*
hold *v., n.*
hole *n.*
holiday *n.*
home *n., adv..*
honest *adj.*
hook *n.*
hope *v., n.*
horn *n.*
horse *n.*
hospital *n.*
hot *adj.*
hotel *n.*
hour *n.*
house *n.*
how *adv.*
however *adv.*
huge *adj.*
human *adj., n.*
humor *n.*
hungry *adj.*
hunt *v.*
hurry *v., n.*
hurt *v.*

husband *n.*

I
I *pron.*
ice *n.*
idea *n.*
identify *v.*
if *conj.*
ignore *v.*
illegal *adj.*
illegally *adv.*
illness *n.*
image *n.*
imagination *n.*
imagine *v.*
immediate *adj.*
immediately *adv.*
impatient *adj.*
importance *n.*
important *adj.*
impossible *adj.*
impress *v.*
impression *n.*
improve *v.*
improvement *n.*
in *prep., adv.*
inch *n.*
include *v.*
including *prep.*
increase *v., n.*
indeed *adv.*
independent *adj.*
individual *adj.*
industry *n.*
infection *n.*
influence *n.*
inform *v.*
informal *adj.*
information *n.*
injure *v.*
injury *n.*
insect *n.*
inside *prep., adv., n., adj.*
instead *adv., prep.*
instruction *n.*
instrument *n.*
insult *v., n.*
intelligent *adj.*
intend *v.*
intention *n.*
interest *n., v.*
interested *adj.*
interesting *adj.*
international *adj.*
Internet *n.*
interrupt *v.*
interview *n.*
into *prep.*
introduce *v.*

introduction *n.*
invent *v.*
investigate *v.*
invitation *n.*
invite *v.*
involve *v.*
iron *n.*
island *n.*
issue *n.*
it *pron.*
item *n.*
its *adj.*
itself *pron.*

J
jacket *n.*
jeans *n.*
jewelry *n.*
job *n.*
join *v.*
joke *n., v.*
judge *n., v.*
judgment *(also*
    judgement) *n.*
juice *n.*
jump *v.*
just *adv.*

K
keep *v.*
key *n.*
kick *v., n.*
kid *n., v.*
kill *v.*
kilogram *(also* kilo) *n.*
kilometer *n.*
kind *n., adj.*
kindness *n.*
king *n.*
kiss *v., n.*
kitchen *n.*
knee *n.*
knife *n.*
knock *v., n.*
knot *n.*
know *v.*
knowledge *n.*

L
lack *n.*
lady *n.*
lake *n.*
lamp *n.*
land *n., v.*
language *n.*
large *adj.*
last *adj., adv., n., v.*
late *adj., adv.*
later *adv.*

laugh *v.*
laundry *n.*
law *n.*
lawyer *n.*
lay *v.*
layer *n.*
lazy *adj.*
lead /lid/ *v.*
leader *n.*
leaf *n.*
lean *v.*
learn *v.*
least *adj., pron., adv.*
    at least
leather *n.*
leave *v.*
left *adj., adv., n.*
leg *n.*
legal *adj.*
legally *adv.*
lemon *n.*
lend *v.*
length *n.*
less *adj., pron., adv.*
lesson *n.*
let *v.*
letter *n.*
level *n.*
library *n.*
lid *n.*
lie *v., n.*
life *n.*
lift *v.*
light *n., adj., v.*
lightly *adv.*
like *prep., v., conj.*
likely *adj.*
limit *n., v.*
line *n.*
lip *n.*
liquid *n., adj.*
list *n., v.*
listen *v.*
liter *n.*
literature *n.*
little *adj., pron., adv.*
    a little
live /lɪv/ *v.*
living *adj.*
load *n., v.*
loan *n.*
local *adj.*
lock *v., n.*
lonely *adj.*
long *adj., adv.*
look *v., n.*
loose *adj.*
lose *v.*
loss *n.*

The Oxford 2000 List of Keywords

lost *adj.*
lot *pron., adv.*
  a lot (of)
  lots (of)
loud *adj.*
loudly *adv.*
love *n., v.*
low *adj., adv.*
luck *n.*
lucky *adj.*
lump *n.*
lunch *n.*

M

machine *n.*
magazine *n.*
magic *n., adj.*
mail *n., v.*
main *adj.*
mainly *adv.*
make *v.*
male *adj., n.*
man *n.*
manage *v.*
manager *n.*
many *adj., pron.*
map *n.*
mark *n., v.*
market *n.*
marriage *n.*
married *adj.*
marry *v.*
match *n., v.*
material *n.*
math *n.*
mathematics *n.*
matter *n., v.*
may *modal v.*
maybe *adv.*
me *pron.*
meal *n.*
mean *v.*
meaning *n.*
measure *v., n.*
measurement *n.*
meat *n.*
medical *adj.*
medicine *n.*
medium *adj.*
meet *v.*
meeting *n.*
melt *v.*
member *n.*
memory *n.*
mental *adj.*
mention *v.*
mess *n.*
message *n.*
messy *adj.*

metal *n.*
method *n.*
meter *n.*
middle *n., adj.*
midnight *n.*
might *modal v.*
mile *n.*
milk *n.*
mind *n., v.*
mine *pron.*
minute *n.*
mirror *n.*
Miss *n.*
miss *v.*
missing *adj.*
mistake *n.*
mix *v.*
mixture *n.*
model *n.*
modern *adj.*
mom *n.*
moment *n.*
money *n.*
month *n.*
mood *n.*
moon *n.*
moral *adj.*
morally *adv.*
more *adj., pron., adv.*
morning *n.*
most *adj., pron., adv.*
mostly *adv.*
mother *n.*
motorcycle *n.*
mountain *n.*
mouse *n.*
mouth *n.*
move *v., n.*
movement *n.*
movie *n.*
Mr. *abbr.*
Mrs. *abbr.*
Ms. *abbr.*
much *adj., pron., adv.*
mud *n.*
multiply *v.*
murder *n., v.*
muscle *n.*
museum *n.*
music *n.*
musical *adj.*
musician *n.*
must *modal v.*
my *adj.*
myself *pron.*
mysterious *adj.*

N

nail *n.*

name *n., v.*
narrow *adj.*
nation *n.*
national *adj.*
natural *adj.*
nature *n.*
navy *n.*
near *adj., adv., prep.*
nearby *adj., adv.*
nearly *adv.*
neat *adj.*
neatly *adv.*
necessary *adj.*
neck *n.*
need *v., n.*
needle *n.*
negative *adj.*
neighbor *n.*
neither *adj., pron., adv.*
nerve *n.*
nervous *adj.*
net *n.*
never *adv.*
new *adj.*
news *n.*
newspaper *n.*
next *adj., adv., n.*
nice *adj.*
night *n.*
no *exclamation, adj.*
nobody *pron.*
noise *n.*
noisy *adj.*
noisily *adv.*
none *pron.*
nonsense *n.*
no one *pron.*
nor *conj.*
normal *adj.*
normally *adv.*
north *n., adj., adv.*
northern *adj.*
nose *n.*
not *adv.*
note *n.*
nothing *pron.*
notice *v.*
novel *n.*
now *adv.*
nowhere *adv.*
nuclear *adj.*
number (*abbr.* No., no.) *n.*
nurse *n.*
nut *n.*

O

object *n.*
obtain *v.*
obvious *adj.*

occasion *n.*
occur *v.*
ocean *n.*
o'clock *adv.*
odd *adj.*
of *prep.*
off *adv., prep.*
offense *n.*
offer *v., n.*
office *n.*
officer *n.*
official *adj., n.*
officially *adv.*
often *adv.*
oh *exclamation*
oil *n.*
OK (*also* okay)
  exclamation, adj., adv.
old *adj.*
old-fashioned *adj.*
on *prep., adv.*
once *adv., conj.*
one *number, adj., pron.*
onion *n.*
only *adj., adv.*
onto *prep.*
open *adj., v..*
operate *v.*
operation *n.*
opinion *n.*
opportunity *n.*
opposite *adj., adv., n., prep.*
or *conj.*
orange *n., adj.*
order *n., v.*
ordinary *adj.*
organization *n.*
organize *v.*
organized *adj.*
original *adj., n.*
other *adj., pron.*
otherwise *adv.*
ought to *modal v.*
ounce *n.*
our *adj.*
ours *pron.*
ourselves *pron.*
out *adj., adv.*
out of *prep.*
outside *n., adj., prep., adv.*
oven *n.*
over *adv., prep.*
owe *v.*
own *adj., pron., v.*
owner *n.*

P

pack *v., n.*
package *n.*

page *n.*
pain *n.*
painful *adj.*
paint *n., v.*
painter *n.*
painting *n.*
pair *n.*
pale *adj.*
pan *n.*
pants *n.*
paper *n.*
parent *n.*
park *n., v.*
part *n.*
   take part (in)
particular *adj.*
particularly *adv.*
partly *adv.*
partner *n.*
party *n.*
pass *v.*
passage *n.*
passenger *n.*
passport *n.*
past *adj., n., prep., adv.*
path *n.*
patient *n., adj.*
pattern *n.*
pause *v.*
pay *v., n.*
payment *n.*
peace *n.*
peaceful *adj.*
pen *n.*
pencil *n.*
people *n.*
perfect *adj.*
perform *v.*
performance *n.*
perhaps *adv.*
period *n.*
permanent *adj.*
permission *n.*
person *n.*
personal *adj.*
personality *n.*
persuade *v.*
pet *n.*
phone *n.*
photo *n.*
photograph *n.*
phrase *n.*
physical *adj.*
physically *adv.*
piano *n.*
pick *v.*
   pick sth up
picture *n.*
piece *n.*

pig *n.*
pile *n.*
pilot *n.*
pin *n.*
pink *adj., n.*
pint *n.*
pipe *n.*
place *n., v.*
   take place
plain *adj.*
plan *n., v.*
plane *n.*
planet *n.*
plant *n., v.*
plastic *n.*
plate *n.*
play *v., n.*
player *n.*
pleasant *adj.*
please *exclamation, v.*
pleased *adj.*
pleasure *n.*
plenty *pron.*
pocket *n.*
poem *n.*
poetry *n.*
point *n., v.*
pointed *adj.*
poison *n., v.*
poisonous *adj.*
police *n.*
polite *adj.*
politely *adv.*
political *adj.*
politician *n.*
politics *n.*
pollution *n.*
pool *n.*
poor *adj.*
popular *adj.*
port *n.*
position *n.*
positive *adj.*
possibility *n.*
possible *adj.*
possibly *adv.*
post *n.*
pot *n.*
potato *n.*
pound *n.*
pour *v.*
powder *n.*
power *n.*
powerful *adj.*
practical *adj.*
practice *n., v.*
prayer *n.*
prefer *v.*
pregnant *adj.*

preparation *n.*
prepare *v.*
present *adj., n., v.*
president *n.*
press *n., v.*
pressure *n.*
pretend *v.*
pretty *adv., adj.*
prevent *v.*
previous *adj.*
price *n.*
priest *n.*
principal *n.*
print *v.*
priority *n.*
prison *n.*
prisoner *n.*
private *adj.*
prize *n.*
probable *adj.*
probably *adv.*
problem *n.*
process *n.*
produce *v.*
product *n.*
production *n.*
professional *adj.*
profit *n.*
program *n.*
progress *n.*
project *n.*
promise *v., n.*
pronunciation *n.*
proof *n.*
proper *adj.*
property *n.*
protect *v.*
protection *n.*
protest *n.*
proud *adj.*
prove *v.*
provide *v.*
public *adj., n.*
   publicly *adv.*
publish *v.*
pull *v.*
punish *v.*
punishment *n.*
pure *adj.*
purple *adj., n.*
purpose *n.*
   on purpose
push *v., n.*
put *v.*

Q
quality *n.*
quantity *n.*
quarter *n.*

queen *n.*
question *n., v.*
quick *adj.*
quickly *adv.*
quiet *adj.*
quietly *adv.*
quite *adv.*

R
race *n., v.*
radio *n.*
railroad *n.*
rain *n., v.*
raise *v.*
rare *adj.*
rarely *adv.*
rate *n.*
rather *adv.*
reach *v.*
reaction *n.*
read *v.*
ready *adj.*
real *adj.*
reality *n.*
realize *v.*
really *adv.*
reason *n.*
reasonable *adj.*
receive *v.*
recent *adj.*
recently *adv.*
recognize *v.*
recommend *v.*
record *n., v.*
recover *v.*
red *adj., n.*
reduce *v.*
refer to *v.*
refuse *v.*
region *n.*
regular *adj.*
regularly *adv.*
relation *n.*
relationship *n.*
relax *v.*
relaxed *adj.*
release *v.*
relevant *adj.*
relief *n.*
religion *n.*
religious *adj.*
rely *v.*
remain *v.*
remark *n.*
remember *v.*
remind *v.*
remove *v.*
rent *n., v.*
repair *v., n.*

repeat v.
replace v.
reply n., v.
report v., n.
reporter n.
represent v.
request n., v.
require v.
rescue v.
research n., v.
reservation n.
respect n., v.
responsibility n.
responsible adj.
rest n., v.
restaurant n.
result n., v.
return v., n.
rice n.
rich adj.
rid v.: get rid of
ride v., n.
right adj., adv., n.
ring n., v.
rise n., v.
risk n., v.
river n.
road n.
rob v.
rock n.
role n.
roll n., v.
romantic adj.
roof n.
room n.
root n.
rope n.
rough adj.
round adj.
route n.
row n.
royal adj.
rub v.
rubber n.
rude adj.
   rudely adv.
ruin v.
rule n., v.
run v., n.
rush v.

S
sad adj.
sadness n.
safe adj.
safely adv.
safety n.
sail v.
salad n.

sale n.
salt n.
same adj., pron.
sand n.
satisfaction n.
satisfied adj.
sauce n.
save v.
say v.
scale n.
scare v.
scared adj.
scary adj.
schedule n.
school n.
science n.
scientific adj.
scientist n.
scissors n.
score n., v.
scratch v., n.
screen n.
search n., v.
season n.
seat n.
second adj., adv., n.
secret adj., n.
secretary n.
secretly adv.
section n.
see v.
seed n.
seem v.
sell v.
send v.
senior adj.
sense n.
sensible adj.
sensitive adj.
sentence n.
separate adj., v.
separately adv.
series n.
serious adj.
serve v.
service n.
set n., v.
settle v.
several adj., pron.
sew v.
sex n.
sexual adj.
shade n.
shadow n.
shake v.
shame n.
shape n., v.
   shaped adj.
share v., n.

sharp adj.
she pron.
sheep n.
sheet n.
shelf n.
shell n.
shine v.
shiny adj.
ship n.
shirt n.
shock n., v.
shoe n.
shoot v.
shop v.
shopping n.
short adj.
shot n.
should modal v.
shoulder n.
shout v., n.
show v., n.
shower n.
shut v.
shy adj.
sick adj.
side n.
sight n.
sign n., v.
signal n.
silence n.
silly adj.
silver n., adj.
similar adj.
simple adj.
since prep., conj., adv.
sing v.
singer n.
single adj.
sink v.
sir n.
sister n.
sit v.
situation n.
size n.
skill n.
skin n.
skirt n.
sky n.
sleep v., n.
sleeve n.
slice n.
slide v.
slightly adv.
slip v.
slow adj.
slowly adv.
small adj.
smell v., n.
smile v., n.

smoke n., v.
smooth adj.
   smoothly adv.
snake n.
snow n., v.
so adv., conj.
soap n.
social adj.
society n.
sock n.
soft adj.
soil n.
soldier n.
solid adj., n.
solution n.
solve v.
some adj., pron.
somebody pron.
somehow adv.
someone pron.
something pron.
sometimes adv.
somewhere adv.
son n.
song n.
soon adv.
   as soon as
sore adj.
sorry adj.
sort n., v.
sound n., v.
soup n.
south n., adj., adv.
southern adj.
space n.
speak v.
speaker n.
special adj.
speech n.
speed n.
spell v.
spend v.
spice n.
spider n.
spirit n.
spoil v.
spoon n.
sport n.
spot n.
spread v.
spring n.
square adj., n.
stage n.
stair n.
stamp n.
stand v., n.
standard n., adj.
star n.
stare v.

start *v., n.*
state *n., v.*
statement *n.*
station *n.*
stay *v.*
steady *adj.*
steal *v.*
steam *n.*
step *n., v.*
stick *v., n.*
sticky *adj.*
still *adv., adj.*
stomach *n.*
stone *n.*
stop *v., n.*
store *n., v.*
storm *n.*
story *n.*
stove *n.*
straight *adv., adj.*
strange *adj.*
street *n.*
strength *n.*
stress *n.*
stretch *v.*
strict *adj.*
string *n.*
strong *adj.*
strongly *adv.*
structure *n.*
struggle *v., n.*
student *n.*
study *n., v.*
stuff *n.*
stupid *adj.*
style *n.*
subject *n.*
substance *n.*
succeed *v.*
success *n.*
successful *adj.*
successfully *adv.*
such *adj.*
   such as
suck *v.*
sudden *adj.*
suddenly *adv.*
suffer *v.*
sugar *n.*
suggest *v.*
suggestion *n.*
suit *n.*
suitable *adj.*
sum *n.*
summer *n.*
sun *n.*
supply *n.*
support *n., v.*
suppose *v.*

sure *adj., adv.*
surface *n.*
surprise *n., v.*
surprised *adj.*
surround *v.*
survive *v.*
swallow *v.*
swear *v.*
sweat *n., v.*
sweet *adj.*
swim *v.*
switch *n., v.*
symbol *n.*
system *n.*

T
table *n.*
tail *n.*
take *v.*
talk *v., n.*
tall *adj.*
tape *n.*
task *n.*
taste *n., v.*
tax *n.*
tea *n.*
teach *v.*
teacher *n.*
team *n.*
tear /tɛr/ *v.*
tear /tɪr/ *n.*
technical *adj.*
technology *n.*
telephone *n.*
television *n.*
tell *v.*
temperature *n.*
temporary *adj.*
tend *v.*
terrible *adj.*
test *n., v.*
text *n.*
than *prep., conj.*
thank *v.*
thanks *n.*
thank you *n.*
that *adj., pron., conj.*
the *definite article*
theater *n.*
their *adj.*
theirs *pron.*
them *pron.*
themselves *pron.*
then *adv.*
there *adv.*
therefore *adv.*
they *pron.*
thick *adj.*
thin *adj.*

thing *n.*
think *v.*
thirsty *adj.*
this *adj., pron.*
though *conj., adv.*
thought *n.*
thread *n.*
threat *n.*
threaten *v.*
throat *n.*
through *prep., adv.*
throw *v.*
thumb *n.*
ticket *n.*
tie *v., n.*
tight *adj., adv.*
time *n.*
tire *n.*
tired *adj.*
title *n.*
to *prep., infinitive marker*
today *adv., n.*
toe *n.*
together *adv.*
toilet *n.*
tomato *n.*
tomorrow *adv., n.*
tongue *n.*
tonight *adv., n.*
too *adv.*
tool *n.*
tooth *n.*
top *n., adj.*
topic *n.*
total *adj., n.*
totally *adv.*
touch *v., n.*
tour *n.*
tourist *n.*
toward *prep.*
towel *n.*
town *n.*
toy *n.*
track *n.*
tradition *n.*
traffic *n.*
train *n., v.*
training *n.*
translate *v.*
transparent *adj.*
transportation *n.*
trash *n.*
travel *v., n.*
treat *v.*
treatment *n.*
tree *n.*
trial *n.*
trick *n.*
trip *n., v.*

trouble *n.*
truck *n.*
true *adj.*
trust *n., v.*
truth *n.*
try *v.*
tube *n.*
tune *n.*
tunnel *n.*
turn *v., n.*
TV *n.*
twice *adv.*
twist *v.*
type *n., v.*
typical *adj.*

U
ugly *adj.*
unable *adj.*
uncle *n.*
uncomfortable *adj.*
unconscious *adj.*
under *prep., adv.*
underground *adj., adv.*
understand *v.*
underwater *adj., adv.*
underwear *n.*
unemployment *n.*
unexpected *adj.*
unexpectedly *adv.*
unfair *adj.*
unfortunately *adv.*
unfriendly *adj.*
unhappy *adj.*
uniform *n.*
union *n.*
unit *n.*
universe *n.*
university *n.*
unkind *adj.*
unknown *adj.*
unless *conj.*
unlikely *adj.*
unlucky *adj.*
unpleasant *adj.*
until *conj., prep.*
unusual *adj.*
up *adv., prep.*
upper *adj.*
upset *v., adj.*
upstairs *adv., adj.*
upward *adv.*
urgent *adj.*
us *pron.*
use *v., n.*
used *adj.*
used to *modal v.*
useful *adj.*
user *n.*

The Oxford 2000 List of Keywords

usual *adj.*
usually *adv.*

V

vacation *n.*
valley *n.*
valuable *adj.*
value *n.*
variety *n.*
various *adj.*
vary *v.*
vegetable *n.*
vehicle *n.*
very *adv.*
video *n.*
view *n.*
violence *n.*
violent *adj.*
virtually *adv.*
visit *v., n.*
visitor *n.*
voice *n.*
volume *n.*
vote *n., v.*

W

wait *v.*
wake (up) *v.*
walk *v., n.*
wall *n.*
want *v.*
war *n.*
warm *adj., v.*
warn *v.*
wash *v.*
waste *v., n., adj.*
watch *v., n.*
water *n.*
wave *n., v.*
way *n.*
we *pron.*
weak *adj.*
weakness *n.*
weapon *n.*
wear *v.*
weather *n.*
website *n.*
wedding *n.*
week *n.*
weekend *n.*
weigh *v.*
weight *n.*
welcome *v.*
well *adv., adj., exclamation*
    as well (as)
west *n., adj., adv.*
western *adj.*
wet *adj.*
what *pron., adj.*

whatever *adj., pron., adv.*
wheel *n.*
when *adv., conj.*
whenever *conj.*
where *adv., conj.*
wherever *conj.*
whether *conj.*
which *pron., adj.*
while *conj., n.*
white *adj., n.*
who *pron.*
whoever *pron.*
whole *adj., n.*
whose *adj., pron.*
why *adv.*
wide *adj.*
wife *n.*
wild *adj.*
will *modal v., n.*
win *v.*
wind /wɪnd/ *n.*
window *n.*
wine *n.*
wing *n.*
winner *n.*
winter *n.*
wire *n.*
wish *v., n.*
with *prep.*
within *prep.*
without *prep.*
woman *n.*
wonder *v.*
wonderful *adj.*
wood *n.*
wooden *adj.*
wool *n.*
word *n.*
work *v., n.*
worker *n.*
world *n.*
worried *adj.*
worry *v.*
worse *adj., adv.*
worst *adj., adv., n.*
worth *adj.*
would *modal v.*
wrap *v.*
wrist *n.*
write *v.*
writer *n.*
writing *n.*
wrong *adj., adv.*

Y

yard *n.*
year *n.*
yellow *adj., n.*
yes *exclamation*

yesterday *adv., n.*
yet *adv.*
you *pron.*
young *adj.*
your *adj.*
yours *pron.*
yourself *pron.*
youth *n.*